D1505762

EXTRAORDINARY PATRIOTS OF THE UNITED STATES OF AMERICA

Colonial Times to Pre-Civil War

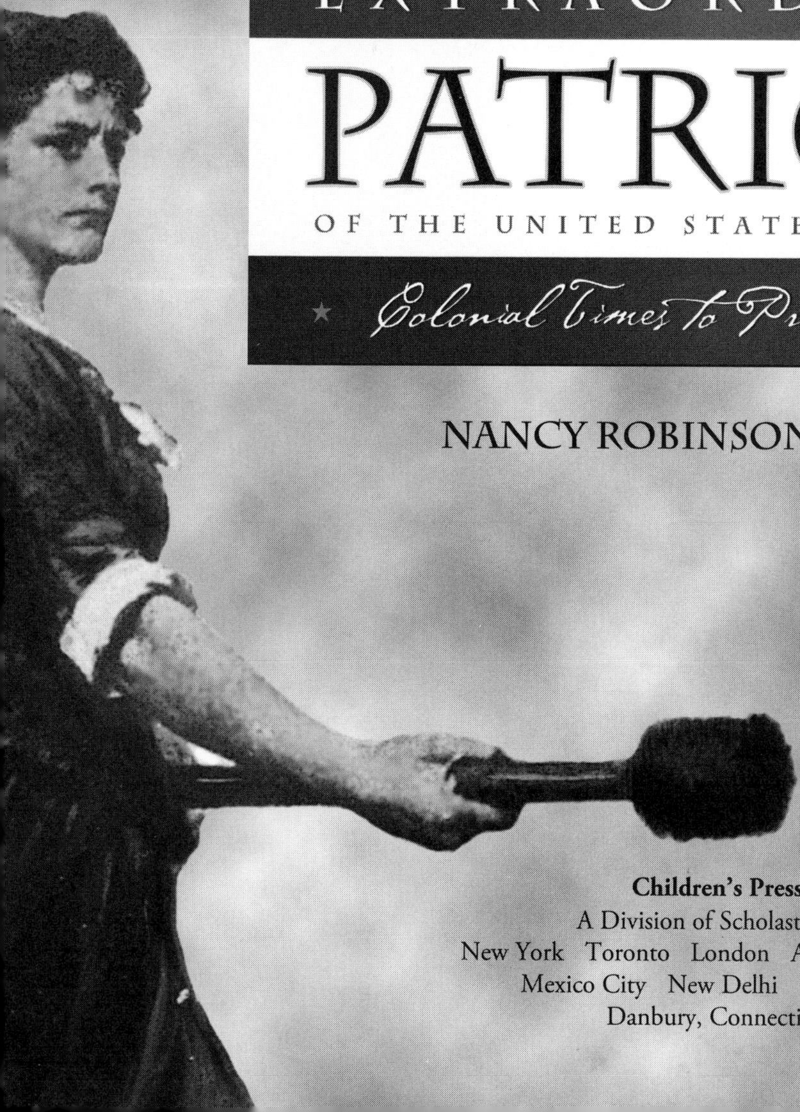

NANCY ROBINSON MASTERS

Children's Press®
A Division of Scholastic Inc.
New York Toronto London Auckland Sydney
Mexico City New Delhi Hong Kong
Danbury, Connecticut

Interior design by Elizabeth Helmetsie

Library of Congress Cataloging-in-Publication Data

Robinson Masters, Nancy.
   Extraordinary patriots of the United States of America: Colonial times to pre–Civil War
/ Nancy Robinson Masters.
      p. cm. — (Extraordinary people)
Includes bibliographical references and index.
ISBN 0–516–24404–3
  1. United States—Biography—Juvenile literature. 2. United States—History—Colonial period,
    ca. 1600–1775—Biography—Juvenile literature. 3. United States—History—Revolution,
    1775–1783—Biography—Juvenile literature. 4. United States—History—1783–1865—
    Biography—Juvenile literature. I. Title. II. Series.
    E176.8.R63 2005
    920.073—dc22   2004030940

1 2 3 4 5 6 7 8 9 10 R 14 13 12 11 10 09 08 07 06 05

CONTENTS

57

George Washington
1732–1799
The Father of Our Country

79

John Hancock
1737–1793
The Man with
the Bold Hand

99

Thomas Jefferson
1743–1826
Architect of Freedom

62

Robert Morris
1734–1806
The Man Who
Financed the Revolution

83

Thomas Paine
1737–1809
The "Common Sense"
Patriot

104

John Jay
1745–1829
First Justice of
the Supreme Court

66

John Adams
1735–1826
Preserver of Liberty

87

Ethan Allen
1738–1789
Leader of the Green
Mountain Boys

108

Benjamin Rush
1745–1813
Surgeon General of
the Continental Army

70

Paul Revere
1735–1818
A Son of Liberty Who
Rode into History

91

Mary Katherine Goddard
1738–1816
First Printer of the Signed
Declaration of Independence

112

Anthony Wayne
1745–1796
Found Wherever
There Was a Fight

75

Patrick Henry
1736–1799
The Son of Thunder

95

Nathanael Greene
1742–1786
Faithful, Fighting General

116

Bernardo de Gálvez
1746–1786
Hispanic Hero
of the Revolution

120
Tadeusz Kosciuszko
1746–1817
Polish Engineer
for Freedom

138
Margaret Cochran Corbin
1751–1800
First Woman Wounded
on the Battlefield

157
Mary Hays McCauley
c. 1754–1832
Molly Pitcher

123
John Paul Jones
1747–1792
Father of the
American Navy

142
James Madison
1751–1836
Champion for
the Constitution

160
Dr. James Thacher
1754–1844
Surgeon, Soldier,
Scribe

126
Casimir Pulaski
1747–1779
Father of the
American Cavalry

146
George Rogers Clark
1752–1818
The "Great Long Knife"

164
Nathan Hale
1755–1776
Schoolteacher Spy

130
Henry Knox
1750–1806
The "Ox" of the
Revolutionary War

150
Betsy Ross
1752–1836
The Woman Behind the
Legend of the Stars and Stripes

168
Alexander Hamilton
1755–1804
Soldier and Statesman

134
The Liberty Bell
1751–Present
A Chime That
Changed the World

154
Jack Jouett
1754–1822
The Other Midnight Rider

173
John Trumbull
1756–1843
Artist of the Revolution

178

Marquis de Lafayette
1757–1834
French Hero of the
American Revolution

182

James Monroe
1758–1831
The Protection
Policy President

186

**Deborah Samson Gannett
(aka Robert Shurtleff)**
1760–1827
Soldier in Disguise

190

Sybil Ludington
1761–1839
Heroine Who
Rode for Freedom

194

Emily Geiger
c. 1763–1825
Legendary Messenger
from South Carolina

198

John Quincy Adams
1767–1848
The President Who
Would Not Quit

202

Andrew Jackson
1767–1845
Hero of
New Orleans

207

Dolley Madison
1768–1849
Patriot of the
People's House

211

African American Patriots
1770–1850
First to Fight for
America's Freedom

215

**Sequoyah
(aka George Gist or Guess)**
c. 1770–1843
Cherokee Warrior

218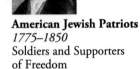

American Jewish Patriots
1775–1850
Soldiers and Supporters
of Freedom

222

George Gibson Jr.
1775–1861
Father of the Army
Food Service

226

Drummers and Fifers
1775–1781
Winning Independence
One Beat at a Time

230

The Oneida
1775–1815
Native American
Patriots

235

**The Declaration
of Independence**
1776–Present
Birth Certificate of the Nation

INTRODUCTION

We mutually pledge to each other our Lives, our Fortunes and our sacred Honor.

—Thomas Jefferson, the Declaration of Independence

What is a patriot? Simply stated, a patriot is a person who loves his or her country and is loyal to its authority. In selecting the *extraordinary* patriots to include in this collection of brief biographies, the definition was more specific: An extraordinary patriot was a person who cared more about establishing and sustaining a free and independent country in America than he or she cared about his or her comfort, safety, property, or life. "Nonperson" patriots that represent these ideals, such as the Purple Heart and the Liberty Bell, were also included in this definition.

The subject of patriotism could be discussed almost anywhere in the time line of human history, but this book has narrowed its focus to one time period:

from just prior to the American Revolution to 1850. The place is similarly narrow: the North American colonies and the United States of America.

The chapters are arranged by birth dates, beginning with Benjamin Franklin, who was born seventy years before the Declaration of Independence was signed, to Sam Houston, born ten years after the end of the Revolutionary War. While it would seem these two very different men born eighty-seven years apart had very little in common, each fits the definition of an extraordinary American patriot during this time.

From the hundreds of suggestions provided by teachers, students, historians, and scholars from across the United States as to who should be included in a book of this scope and size, three categories emerged: well-known, little-known, and unknown patriots who in only one way or in many ways exhibited extraordinary patriotism at a crucial moment in U.S. history.

Soldiers, sailors, and spies were not the only kinds of patriots selected from the hundreds recommended. Painters, printers, and politicians are also included. Among them are George Gibson Jr., who used his pencil to keep the U.S. Army fed for forty-three years, and Jacob Shallus, who used his quill to record the words of the U.S. Constitution on four pieces of parchment.

Other patriots include American frontier soldiers, such as "Mad" Anthony Wayne and George Rogers Clark; and foreign-born fighters such as the Marquis de Lafayette from France, Tadeusz Kosciuszko from Poland, and Friedrich von Steuben from what is now Germany; and women, such as Margaret Corbin, Sybil Ludington, and Mercy Otis Warren, who by virtue of their sex were denied the rights of full citizenship in the country they helped to establish.

The country these well-known, little-known, and unknown patriots established was not perfect. Nor were they perfect in their actions to ensure its survival. For example, some of the framers of the Declaration of Independence and the U.S. Constitution argued publicly for laws to abolish slavery in the United States but at the same time were slaveholders unwilling to abolish slavery in their own homes.

These biographies do not try to accuse or excuse individuals whose attitudes and actions would be in conflict with the current attitudes, culture, and society of the United States. There is not sufficient space to explain the depth and complexity of every issue in every life. To do so would detract from the focus of the patriotic contributions of the subjects during the times and circumstances in which they lived.

Each profile in this book stands alone; it is not necessary to read the book from the beginning as a narrative. The reader may choose to learn about George Washington, the first president of the United States, who appears early in the book, and then skip to the end of the book to compare him with Zachary Taylor, the last president featured. Taylor is the perfect president to conclude with because it was he who held the states together as one nation when the slavery issue threatened to end what Washington and countless others had fought to establish.

Names that appear in bold type within the text are the subjects of their own profiles in separate chapters in the book. Again, this allows the reader to read selected portions without loss of continuity.

Information sources for the most prominent patriots are abundant. Published histories and biographies cover their lives in great detail. While every effort has been made to ensure accuracy, equally reliable sources occasionally produced conflicting information. For some of the more obscure patriots, oral histories published as family recollections had to suffice. Some extraordinary patriots left little written evidence of their lives, including African American patriots who served in wars to buy their freedom and then were sent back to slavery and never had the opportunity to document their patriotism.

It is hoped the reader will discover a fresh appreciation for these patriots who made it possible for us to have the extraordinary freedoms we enjoy today in the United States of America.

BENJAMIN FRANKLIN

THE WISE AND WITTY FOUNDING FATHER
1706–1790

We, the people of the United States of America . . .

—Benjamin Franklin,
the preamble to the U.S. Constitution

On September 17, 1787, Jacob Shallus's hand trembled as he began to read aloud the words eighty-one-year-old Benjamin Franklin had dictated to be engrossed (written) as the introduction (preamble) to the **Constitution of the United States of America:** "We, the people," Shallus read. These three words were the birthmark that would identify the United States of America.

Writer, inventor, and patriot, Benjamin Franklin helped create and sign both the **Declaration of Independence** and the Constitution of the United States. He was born in Boston on January 17, 1706, to Josiah Franklin and his second wife, Abiah Folger. Josiah was a chandler (a maker of soap and candles) but did not earn much money. When Benjamin was eight years old, his father sent him to elementary school, hoping a formal education would encourage the young boy to pursue a career as a clergyman.

Benjamin had no interest in becoming a minister. His formal education ended by the time he was ten; his rise from poverty to power began at the age of twelve, when he went to work as an apprentice printer for his brother. Soon Benjamin became an accomplished printer.

Reading during every spare moment in the print shop, young Benjamin fed his hungry mind better than his body. Franklin later wrote that he became a vegetarian partly to save money and buy more books.

When he was seventeen, Franklin ran away to Philadelphia, where he again found work as a printer. His life took a dramatic turn when the governor of Pennsylvania encouraged him to go to England to buy printing equipment. Unfortunately, the money the governor promised to provide for the equipment never arrived. Franklin spent two years working in London before he returned to Philadelphia, bringing back with him a wealth of experiences and enough money to buy a partnership in *The Pennsylvania Gazette*. Not long after, he owned all of the newspaper and was elected the official printer of the state.

When flames destroyed the southern part of Philadelphia, Franklin became a powerful voice urging fire-protection programs. He also drew up the articles of association for The Library Company, the first lending library in the country. He wanted others to share the pleasure he enjoyed through reading.

In December 1732 Franklin brought out the first edition of a series of

Benjamin Franklin (center) learned the trade of printing at an early age.

publications that was to make him rich as well as famous. *Poor Richard's Almanac* entertained readers while also providing information on a wide variety of subjects. Writing as Poor Richard Saunders, Franklin covered everything from weather predictions to wedding advice. Each book was filled with jokes and snappy sayings. Some of Poor Richard's proverbs are still used today, such as "Don't throw stones at your neighbor's house if your own windows are glass" and "Early to bed, early to rise, makes a man healthy, wealthy, and wise."

At a time when the entire population of the United States was less than 3 million people, Franklin was selling ten thousand copies a year of his almanac. He became the official printer for New Jersey as well as Pennsylvania and moved steadily toward becoming one of the colonies' leading publishers. He married Deborah Read in 1730. They had three children: William, Sally, and Francis.

Franklin was a scientist, an inventor, a talented writer, and a creative thinker. His famous kite experiment, in which he tied a metal key to a kite and sent it aloft to be struck by lightning, proved the existence of electricity. Bifocal glasses, the Franklin stove, and other practical items were products of his inventive mind. He filled hundreds of pages with his opinions, essays, and humorous words expressing ideas that were wise as well as witty and that made him an influential community leader. At various times he served as the clerk of the Pennsylvania Assembly and the postmaster of Philadelphia. He organized the first municipal fire department and was one of the founders of the University of Pennsylvania.

As tensions with England increased, Franklin directed his fierce energy and influence to the cause of freedom for the American colonies. He used words as effectively as others used swords. After he signed the Declaration of Independence, he traveled to Paris as one of the commissioners of Congress to the French court. The people of Paris loved Franklin, and he persuaded the French people and government to support the American Revolution with loans, donations, and military supplies. He personally supervised shipments to America from French ports. Ellen Cohn, editor of *The Papers of Benjamin Franklin*, says, "French support was due entirely to Franklin." His talents with negotiating treaties and trade agreements were nothing short of miraculous.

"There never was a good war, or a bad peace," he wrote to **James Madison** in 1783, the year he, along with **John Adams** and **John Jay**, negotiated the Treaty of Peace with Great Britain.

Franklin, the oldest delegate at the Constitutional Convention, presided over its daily meetings. Some of the other delegates were battle-seasoned soldiers, but they looked to Franklin as their leader. He was so ill that he had to be carried into the meeting hall in his chair, which was something like a modern recliner.

His illness made no difference. He missed only three sessions during the four months of meetings in Philadelphia in 1787.

The temperature inside the room "often rose far above that on the outside," Franklin admitted. When tempers flared and angry words from the delegates were directed at him, Franklin would pretend his loss of hearing prevented him from knowing what was being said. "How can I be offended by what I cannot hear?" he would ask with a sly smile.

Along with his patriotic accomplishments, Franklin is also remembered for his tremendous sense of humor. "There would have been no United States Constitution had it not been for Benjamin Franklin's wit," said **Charles Thomson**, one of the other delegates to the Constitutional Convention.

Franklin lived long enough to see the Constitution ratified (accepted) in 1788. He died April 17, 1790, at the age of eighty-four, and was buried beside Deborah, who had died 25 years earlier. More than twenty thousand mourners attended his funeral. His simple tombstone at Philadelphia's Christ Church burial ground is engraved exactly as he requested in his will: "Benjamin and Deborah Franklin: 1790." It makes no mention of his career as a printer and a statesman.

ROGER SHERMAN

THE SHOEMAKER WHO BECAME THE SIGNER
1721–1793

He stood as firm in the cause for independence as Mount Atlas.

—John Adams

Roger Sherman was a hardworking shoemaker who did not attend grammar school until he was thirteen. He became the only man to sign the four most important documents in America's history: the Declaration of the Rights of Colonists (1774), the **Declaration of Independence** (1776), the Articles of Confederation (1777), and the **Constitution of the United States of America** (1787).

Sherman was born in Newton, Massachusetts, on April 19, 1721. His parents, William and Mehetable Wellington Sherman, were not well-to-do, but his father had a good collection of books and taught Roger to read while he worked in the family cordwainer, or shoemaker shop. When his family moved to the town of Stoughton, Roger attended the new grammar school for a short time. His reading skills were far beyond those of the other students, so he left the school to study privately with Samuel Danbar, a minister. Danbar encouraged him to study history, religion, mathematics, law, and astronomy.

When his father died in 1741, Roger continued working as a shoemaker. He did not earn enough money to care for his mother and younger brothers. He put his tools on his back in 1743 and walked to New Milford, Connecticut, where his older brother William lived. That year his superb mathematics skills earned him the job of county surveyor. He earned enough money to exchange making shoes for selling them as the owner of the only store in New Milford.

Sherman married Elizabeth Hartwell in 1749, and they had seven children. Following Elizabeth's death, he married Rebecca Prescott, and they had eight children.

Between 1750 and 1761 Sherman wrote and published a series of almanacs. These were popular publications that contained information about the stars, the planets, and weather that were important not only to farmers but also to businessmen and housewives. People during this period relied on the almanac's information for everything from what time to open and close their shops to when to wash their hair! Unlike the almanacs written by **Benjamin Franklin**, Sherman's did not contain snappy sayings or witty advice.

Sherman's passion for knowledge led him to study law. Without formal training, he passed the Connecticut bar examination and was soon elected to the Connecticut General Assembly. He became known for his straight-across-the-forehead haircut and his careful attention to details. He served as the treasurer of Yale University and received an honorary master of arts degree from the school. Sherman considered this one of his greatest honors.

His reputation as a believer in America's right to govern itself combined with his humble upbringing made Sherman popular with the other colonists who sought independence. In 1774 he was elected to be a delegate (representative) from Connecticut to the First Continental Congress. He joined other members on October 14 in signing the Declaration of the Rights of Colonists. This was the first list the congress wrote stating its complaints about British laws and actions.

When the heated debates of the summer of 1776 began to swing in favor of independence from British rule, Sherman was appointed to the Committee of Five. The other committee members were Benjamin Franklin, **Thomas Jefferson**, **John Adams**, and Robert Livingston. They were assigned the task of writing the formal declaration for independence. The "sturdy Sherman," as Franklin described him, began every day with prayer and then tackled his responsibilities. Nothing distracted him. Jefferson, the primary author of the declaration, listened to Sherman's suggestions, particularly his recommendation that the document express in a logical and orderly manner specific reasons the colonists should be independent. Jefferson knew there was nothing more important to Sherman than the union of the colonies. While making introductions one day in Philadelphia, Jefferson pointed toward the dignified delegate and said, "That is Mr. Sherman of Connecticut, a man who never said a foolish thing in his life."

When the Revolutionary War ended, Sherman signed the Articles of Confederation, which governed the United States between 1781 and 1789. During these years he had more time to focus on his job as a judge for the Superior Court of Connecticut—a position he had held since 1766 and kept for nineteen years.

In 1787, Sherman eagerly went to Philadelphia as a delegate to the Constitutional Convention. He was still the plain-dressed, plain-speaking man who had not forgotten his humble beginnings. He was no longer satisfied, however, merely to add his support to someone else's ideas. Sherman designed the voting plan that assured smaller states such as Connecticut as much of a voice in the nation as the larger states. According to his plan, each state would have two senators. The number of representatives would be based on each state's population. **James Madison**'s notes show that Sherman gave 138 speeches during the convention!

Roger Sherman's familiar signature on the Constitution gave him the distinction no other patriot could claim: he had signed the Declaration of the Rights of Colonists, the Declaration of Independence, the Articles of Confederation, and the Constitution of the United States of America.

At the time of his death on July 23, 1793, Sherman was serving as a senator from Connecticut in the U.S. Senate. He is buried in Grove Street Cemetery in New Haven, Connecticut. The cemetery is listed on the National Register of Historic Places as a National Historic Landmark.

SAMUEL ADAMS

THE SON OF LIBERTY
1722–1803

He stirred men's souls.

—John Adams

On the morning of March 6, 1770, Samuel Adams stood before the British governor of Massachusetts. Only a day earlier British troops had killed five colonists in what would become known as the Boston Massacre.

"Both regiments or none!" insisted Adams as the courageous spokesman for the mob of five thousand colonists demanding the withdrawal of British troops. Reluctantly the governor agreed, and Adams became the hero of Boston.

Samuel Adams was born in Boston on September 27, 1722, to Samuel and Mary Fifield Adams. He was one of twelve children. His father was a wealthy leader of the city. Young Samuel attended the Boston Latin School, then Harvard College, where he earned a master's degree when he was twenty-one.

His father wanted him to be a minister, but Samuel wanted to be a lawyer. His mother objected because the legal profession was not well respected at that time. Samuel went to work for a merchant and later, with a loan from his father, opened his own business. It failed. He went into partnership with his father in the brewing business, but the partnership did not prove to be successful either. When unfair British laws in the colonies caused his father to lose his wealth in a banking venture, Adams began to support the rights of the colonists. As Boston's tax collector, he gained the friendship of nearly every working person in the city by working behind the scenes on their behalf.

His plain dress, shrewd mind, and unusual skill as a writer also helped Adams win the trust of many colonists. He could take very complex issues and make them simple for readers to understand.

Elizabeth Checkley and Samuel Adams were married in 1749. She died in 1757. Adams married Elizabeth Wells in 1764. That same year he entered politics whole-heartedly. The following year he wrote the first public protest in America against the Stamp Act. This act required the colonists to pay a fee to have every document stamped by a British official. Adams insisted that this tax was illegal and began a fierce campaign in Boston that influenced other colonists to resist the tax. When the Stamp Act was repealed in 1766, Adams saw it as a victory for the united efforts of the common citizens.

Adams formed and led a secret society known as the Sons of Liberty. Some members of the group harassed British officials by vandalizing their homes and destroying their property. Not all the colonists favored these extreme actions—some, like **Benjamin Franklin** and **James Otis**, thought the solution to the problems between the colonies and the British might be for the American

Samuel Adams and the Sons of Liberty dumped tea into Boston Harbor in 1773 to protest the tax on tea.

colonies to have representatives in Britain's Parliament. Adams did not want representation in Parliament; he wanted independence. On December 16, 1773, he led a band of about fifty members of the Sons of Liberty disguised as Mohawk Indians aboard British ships in Boston Harbor, where they heaved 342 cases of tea overboard to protest unfair British trade practices. This bold act of defiance earned Adams both friends and foes among the colonists.

Adams created a plan for each community to have a Committee of Correspondence to share information about the actions of the British troops and officials. He urged that a Continental Congress be called to unify the colonies; once one was formed, he was elected a delegate (representative) from Massachusetts. He served for nine years along with his father's cousin, **John Adams**.

For all of his reputation as a troublemaker, Samuel Adams knew how to draw people together for a common cause with his words, his actions, and his emotions. When a delegate suggested that each session of the Congress be opened with a prayer, **John Jay** objected, saying, "Episcopalians, Congregationalists, Presbyterians, Baptists, and Quakers could hardly be expected to unite in formal worship." Adams quickly said he had no problem listening to an Episcopalian pray, "especially an Episcopalian like Mr. Duché of Philadelphia." Adams knew Jacob Duché was a well-known patriot "with whom even the heathen could not find fault." The argument ended, and Duché came to lead the prayers.

Adams's luck appeared to run out in April 1775, when the British soldiers were ordered to arrest him and **John Hancock**. They were to be put on a ship and sent to London to be tried as traitors. Thanks to the efforts of **Paul Revere** and other members of the Sons of Liberty, word reached Lexington, Massachusetts, where the two men were staying, and they escaped.

No one worked harder than Samuel Adams to see America declare independence. He often angered other members of Congress, who saw him as a troublemaker when he did not get his way. He was among the fifty-six delegates who signed the **Declaration of Independence**, the formal announcement of the colonies' separation from British rule, and he continued to serve in Congress until 1781, when he returned to Boston to help the new state government of Massachusetts.

In 1788 Adams was a member of the Massachusetts convention considering ratification (acceptance) of the **Constitution of the United States of America**. A constitution is a set of rules and laws that tells how a government is to be organized and run. Adams was opposed to the Constitution, because he feared it would give too much power to the federal government and did not adequately protect the rights of individuals, until he heard his old friend John Hancock speak in favor of it. Adams then dedicated himself to seeing it ratified. He later worked to include the first ten amendments to ensure the freedoms of individual citizens. These amendments became known as the Bill of Rights.

From 1794 to 1797, Adams served as the governor of Massachusetts. An observer described Adams at seventy-two as "a man with dark blue eyes under bushy brows. He wears plain clothes with buckled shoes, knee breeches, and a red cloak." When asked which he considered to be the most important—the Declaration of Independence or the U.S. Constitution—he would briskly answer, "What is one without the other?"

Adams died on October 2, 1803, at his home in Boston. He is buried in the Granary Burial Grounds.

GEORGE MASON

THE FORGOTTEN FOUNDING FATHER
1725–1792

*ur all is at stake.*

—George Mason

Though he never signed the **Constitution of the United States of America**, George Mason had more to do with its creation than almost any other American.

George Mason was born in Fairfax County, Virginia, in 1725, to George and Ann Mason. When he was ten years old, his father died in a sailboat accident, and his uncle, John

Mercer, became his guardian. Mason never had any formal education, but he avidly read books from Mercer's 1,500-volume library. Many of the books dealt with law, and Mason became a student of politics.

Mason later inherited Gunston Hall, a large Virginia plantation. He became one of Virginia's richest farmers by managing every detail of the plantation's operation. He even supervised the mixing of the lime and sand used as plaster on the house to eliminate cockroaches.

In 1750 Mason married Anne Eilbeck, with whom he had five sons and four daughters. She died in 1773 at the age of thirty-nine. Seven years later he married Sarah Brent of Stafford County, Virginia.

Mason bought into the Ohio Company in 1752. The company's purpose was to develop western lands, but Britain did not want the colonists to expand their landholdings. During the next twenty years the colonists rebelled against the British government, and Britain revoked the rights of the Ohio Company. In 1774 Mason helped write the Fairfax Resolves, in which the colonists protested a law that denied them use of Boston Harbor.

When the Continental Congress elected **George Washington** as commander in chief of the Continental army in 1775, Mason took his place in the Virginia legislature. He was hesitant to take the position, but he soon earned respect for his thoroughness and wisdom. Both qualities were evident in his writing of the Virginia Declaration of Rights in 1776. **Thomas Jefferson** used the first part of Mason's declaration (statement of beliefs) as a model for the United States' **Declaration of Independence**. Mason's most important contribution to America was to specify in his declaration that government's role should be limited in favor of the rights of individuals.

Because his love of liberty was greater than his dislike of politics, Mason stayed in the Virginia legislature. He worked to pass laws to help the colonists in the War of Independence, though he often complained of various illnesses and was usually late for meetings. He particularly disliked "babblers," whom he said "talked much, but said little." Mason also talked much, but those who listened agreed that what he said was essential. In fact, Jefferson considered him the "wisest man of his generation."

Mason grew so disgusted with the babblers that he retired from politics in 1780. He swore he would never return to public service. He agreed, however, to be a delegate to the 1787 Constitutional Convention in Philadelphia. The purpose of the convention was to revise the Articles of Confederation, which had governed the United States since 1776. Mason feared the federal government would be given too much power in the new Constitution of the United States of America. Yet he did agree that the Articles of Confederation were not strong enough to hold the states together as one country. In a letter to one of his sons, he included a prayer that God would grant the delegates the ability to establish "a wise and just government."

Mason introduced many of the ideas that were written into the Constitution. He supported dividing the government into three branches to keep any one branch from having more power than the other. Although he owned many slaves, Mason campaigned for the Constitution to outlaw slavery and to contain a list of "inalienable" rights. These were natural rights, Mason said, that could not be taken away from people by any government. Mason had already made 137 speeches to the other delegates when, on September 12, 1787, he rose one more time to propose that a "bill of rights" protecting individual citizens be included as part of the rules and laws of the government. To his dismay, all the other delegates voted against his proposal!

Mason refused to sign the final version of the Constitution on September 17, 1787. His decision surprised everyone, especially his longtime friend and fellow Virginia delegate George Washington. Mason's refusal to sign ended their friendship. Mason told the other Virginia delegate, **James Madison**, that he did not sign the Constitution because it created a federal government that would be too powerful, it did not end the slave trade, and it did not contain a bill of rights.

Mason joined with **Patrick Henry** to lead the anti-Federalists in opposing ratification (acceptance) of the Constitution. Newspaper articles supporting the Constitution written under the pen name **Publius** began appearing, so Mason wrote opposing articles. Publius's articles, written by **John Jay**, **Alexander Hamilton**, and Madison, succeeded in helping the Constitution of the United States of America become ratified in 1788.

In the first session of the first Congress meeting under the new Constitution, James Madison introduced a bill of rights very much like Mason's. After learning that the first ten amendments to the Constitution, known as the Bill of Rights, were accepted, Mason told Madison he could now "cheerfully accept" the new government, although the amendment to end slavery would not be added for many more years.

Mason lost many friends in the battle over the Constitution, but he also gained many admirers. Some, like Jefferson, continued to visit him until he died on October 7, 1792. He is buried at Gunston Hall plantation.

JAMES OTIS

COLONIAL AMERICA'S FLAME OF FIRE
1725–1783

The only principles of public conduct worthy of a man are . . . the sacred calls of his country.

—James Otis

A lawyer, speaker, and political leader, James Otis stepped forward to defend America's rights in the pre–Revolutionary War period. He was impulsive, sincere, enthusiastic, and devoted to truth and justice.

Otis was born February 5, 1725, in West Barnstable, Massachusetts. He was one of thirteen children born to well-known political leader James Otis, Sr. and his wife, Mary Allyne Otis. His sister, **Mercy Otis Warren**, later wrote a three-volume history of the Revolutionary War.

Five years after Otis graduated from Harvard College in 1743, he was licensed to practice law in Massachusetts. In 1755 he married Ruth Cunningham, the daughter of a Boston merchant. His superb legal skills led to his appointment as advocate general to the British Crown, which was a very important and well-paying position for a colonist.

In 1760 the British government renewed the laws known as the Writs of Assistance. These gave British officers the right to search any business or private place for any reason. The British knew some colonial merchants were smuggling goods without paying taxes, and they felt the writs were justified. Colonists, however, were angered by the laws.

As advocate general to the crown, Otis was required to uphold these writs. Instead, he refused to support the customs officers and resigned his position. In 1761 England took the colonists to court over their opposition to the writs. The colonists immediately sought Otis's help in resisting the Writs of Assistance.

In a courtroom before British judges, Otis spoke for five hours about mankind's natural rights to life, liberty, and property.

"Otis was a flame of fire," **John Adams** wrote in his notes on Otis's speech. "Then and there the child Independence was born."

In 1765 Otis spoke out against the Stamp Act, which required the colonists to pay to have every document stamped by a British official. Otis angrily encouraged the colonists to move toward freedom. He preached that "taxation without representation" was cruel and unjust, convincing not only others but also himself that independence was necessary.

Otis's speeches made him many enemies among British officials and colonists loyal to British rule. One night in 1769, John Robinson, a British court commissioner, attacked Otis in a coffeehouse with his cane. Robinson cracked

Otis's skull, causing serious brain damage from which he never completely recovered. On one occasion in 1770, Otis lost control of his emotions in the Massachusetts State House and began breaking windows, burning papers, and firing off a rifle. He was judged a "lunatic," but the people still wanted him to represent them in the legislature. At a town meeting in Boston later that year, the colonists gave a resolution of thanks to Otis, wishing for his recovery and asking that his name always be listed "among the Patriots of America."

In the years after the attack, Otis's mind often played tricks on him, though patriotism still burned within his soul. On the evening of June 17, 1775, he slipped away from his sister's home where he was staying and fell in with a group of soldiers marching to fight at Bunker Hill. He managed to find his way back to his sister's home that night, unaware of where he had been.

As Otis's mental state worsened, he repeatedly said he hoped God would take him out "by a flash of lightning." On May 23, 1783, that happened in Andover, Massachusetts. One version of the incident says he was struck by a bolt of lightning while standing inside a doorway watching a storm. Another says he was standing outside by a fence giving a "speech" to neighbors when he was struck and killed instantly. He is buried in the Granary Burying Grounds in Boston.

A bronze plaque placed on his grave in 1898 reads "James Otis, Orator and Patriot of the Revolution." Almost a hundred years later a bronze statue was erected in his honor in front of the Barnstable County Courthouse. The words of an elderly John Adams, however, are probably the tribute Otis would most enjoy: "I have never known a man whose love of country was more sincere."

CAESAR RODNEY

DELAWARE HERO IN THE VOTE FOR INDEPENDENCE

1728–1784

 *vote for independence.*

—Caesar Rodney, July 2, 1776

Sweat dropped from Caesar Rodney's chin to the horse's neck beneath him. The cancer on his thin face had begun to take its toll, but tonight his usually pale skin was flushed. All that he had worked for was at stake. Even the painful memories of his courtship of Molly Vining, who had refused his attentions and married another man, could not distract him from his mission

to ensure that Delaware voted for independence.

Rodney was born on October 7, 1728, on his father's farm in Dover, Delaware. The oldest of eight children, he was tutored by his parents and had no formal schooling until he was fourteen, when he went to Philadelphia to attend school. Three years later his father died, and the Kent County, Delaware, clerk of the peace became Caesar's guardian. His guardian's knowledge of the law led Rodney to want to work in a public-service job. From his election as the high sheriff of Kent County to his election as a delegate (representative) to the Continental Congress in Philadelphia, Rodney dedicated himself to every duty he was given with such enthusiasm that **John Adams** described him as someone with "a sense of fire, spirit, wit and humor."

On the afternoon of June 30, 1776, the Continental Congress took the first vote on a motion for independence. Nine of the colonies voted for independence, two voted against, and New York did not vote. The thirteenth colony, Delaware, was undecided. One of its three delegates voted for and one delegate voted against. The third Delaware delegate was Caesar Rodney, who was not in Philadelphia, where the Continental Congress was meeting in secret. Now a brigadier general in the Delaware militia (citizen soldiers), he had remained at home to deal with an uprising of the Loyalists, the supporters of the British in America. A second vote would be taken on July 2.

Delaware delegate Thomas McKean sent a frantic message to Rodney: "Come at once. Your vote is desperately needed."

Riding eighty miles by horse in one day to get to Philadelphia in time for the vote would be grueling for a young man. Rodney was forty-eight, had severe asthma, and was suffering from facial cancer. Undaunted, he was determined to reach Philadelphia in time to vote for independence. "It was either dependence or independence," he later wrote.

On the evening of July 1, 1776, Rodney climbed into the saddle to make the journey. Time was short. A wild thunderstorm with heavy downpours and blinding lightning flashes crashed upon him as he traveled over mud-filled roads and crossed unsteady bridges above rising streams. Rodney ignored the pain in his face from the cancer sores, struggling to breathe as he rode through the night without stopping.

Late on the afternoon of July 2, the mud-covered and exhausted Rodney rode up to the hall where the meetings of the Congress were being held. He arrived in time to hear the last minutes of debate on the independence motion before the second vote was taken. When his time to vote came, Rodney, near collapse and still wearing his spurs, made the declaration, "I vote *for* independence." With this vote, Delaware joined the other colonies that had declared their independence from British rule.

Rodney returned to Delaware after the vote, joined with General **George Washington**'s forces, and was named commander of the post at Trenton. Washington praised Rodney for his success in the assigned operation, and his rank was raised to major general of the Delaware militia.

By the time the Revolutionary War ended, Rodney had earned the title "Delaware's Hero." He won election to the Delaware General Assembly hoping to serve the people for whom he had helped win independence, although he was never seen without his face wrapped in a green silk scarf that he wore to conceal the ugly ravages of the cancer.

By 1784 the lack of treatment for his cancer and his asthma left Rodney too ill to attend the assembly meetings, but this did not end his public service. He was so respected that the assembly decided to hold its meetings in his home.

Rodney never married. He died on his Delaware farm in late June, 1784. For more than a hundred years his grave went unmarked, but in 1889 his remains were moved to Christ Churchyard in Dover, Delaware, where a monument honors him.

In 1999 the Delaware quarter became the first coin released by the U.S. Mint's Fifty State Quarters program. The Delaware quarter's reverse image depicts Caesar Rodney riding his galloping horse to cast the deciding vote for independence.

MERCY OTIS WARREN

FIRST LADY OF THE REVOLUTION
1728-1814

*M*s. *Warren used pen and paper to champion the cause of independence.*

—*Cape Cod Times*, 2000

Mercy Otis Warren became the first published female author in colonial America whose plays and other writings openly criticized British rulers. Her goal was to see the American colonies free from British rule, and her pursuit of this goal made her one of the early political activists for women's rights in America.

"Without this freedom," she told a group gathered in her home in 1772, "there is no hope for women to ever reach their rightful place as full citizens in America."

Mercy was born in 1728, the third child of James and Mary Allyne Otis. Her ancestors were some of the earliest Pilgrim settlers. The Otis family lived in Barnstable, Massachusetts, a town south of Plymouth on Cape Cod where her father was a farmer, merchant, and attorney. His successful law practice played a major role in his election to the Massachusetts House of Representatives. "Politics were my playmates while growing up in Barnstable," Mercy said.

Her father wanted his sons to have an education, so he hired the Reverend Jonathan Russell to prepare **James** and Joseph for college. When Joseph decided against attending college, Mercy took his place in the classroom. She became a superior student, with history her favorite subject.

Both James and Mercy proved to be excellent writers and speakers. These skills allowed them to influence many others to want independence from the tyranny (unjust rule) of Britain's king.

At the age of twenty-six, Mercy married James Warren, a Harvard classmate of her brother. Some believe Mercy's "late" marriage was another indication of her love of independence, since most women in those days married well before their twenty-first birthday.

While her husband served in the colonial legislature and became a leader in revolutionary politics, Mercy took care of their five sons; however, she did not stop writing and speaking in support of America's freedom. The Warren home became a common meeting place for revolutionaries (people in favor of independence from Britain). Mercy was frequently the only woman present, and she was not hesitant to participate in political discussions.

Mercy developed close friendships with Abigail and **John Adams**. For a time Mercy and John were not on good terms after he took offense at some of her remarks, but eventually the two became friends again.

A tragedy in 1769 led to Mercy becoming even more influential as a "blue-stocking," as women writers were called. A British officer whom James Otis had called a liar viciously attacked him. The beating left Otis mentally disabled. Friends, including John Adams, urged Mercy to take James's place in speaking out for independence. "Tell your wife," Adams wrote to Mercy's husband, "God Almighty has entrusted her with Powers for the good of the world, which He bestows on few of the human race."

From that day forward Mercy Otis Warren devoted her "powers" to the revolutionary cause. Words that poured from her quill onto paper were printed in newspapers everywhere. Her name, however, did not appear with her writing because of the risk of British retaliation.

In 1790 Warren began publishing her writings in her own name: Mrs. M. Warren. In her poems and plays women were shown as public speakers and rebel leaders, causing some to disapprove of her writings. These critics were unaware that Warren's most important writing had not yet been published, though she had been working on it for many years. Her "I was there" account of the Revolution, titled *History of the Rise, Progress, and Termination of the American Revolution*, was published beginning in 1805 and filled three volumes with more than 1,100 pages. These volumes are still considered one of the most vivid records of America's fight for independence, although some historians have debated their accuracy.

Warren died on October 19, 1814. A life-size bronze statue of her stands on the front lawn of the Barnstable County Courthouse opposite that of her brother, James. It honors her as the "First Lady of the American Revolution."

CHARLES THOMSON

THE MAN WHO TOLD THE TRUTH
1729–1824

f the truth were known, the leadership of the nation would be weakened.

—Charles Thomson

Charles Thomson looked at the piles of papers in front of him. From 1774 until 1789, he had carefully recorded every word, every action, and every decision made by the Continental Congress and the Congress of the United States of America. From those records he had written a book, a truthful account of what had really happened during the proceedings. The book did not skip over the dark, ugly moments Thomson had witnessed. It was so honest, he feared what future generations would think after reading it.

Now in his ninety-fifth year, Thomson knew he had to make a decision. His wife was dead, and he had no children. What should he do with this manuscript?

Charles Thomson was born in Londonderry, now called Derry, Ireland, on November 29, 1729. As a child he helped his father bleach linen in their family cloth business. When Thomson's mother died in 1739, his father booked passage for the family on a ship to America. His father died on the ship just before it reached Delaware. His oldest brother could not care for Charles, so he was placed with a blacksmith as an apprentice (someone who worked with a tradesman to learn a skill). Charles was unhappy and ran away from the blacksmith. Dr. Francis Allison, later an administrator at Philadelphia College, took Charles into his school in New London, Pennsylvania. He progressed quickly and became the principal of a Society of Friends (Quaker) academy.

Thomson's ability to keep a secret made him a trusted friend to **Benjamin Franklin**, **Thomas Jefferson**, and other prominent Philadelphia citizens. In 1757 he was part of a Quaker council attempting to resolve a twenty-year-old land war with the Delaware (Lenape) Indians. Thomson's investigations at the request of the king of England into the "walking purchase" revealed how some colonists had cheated the Delaware tribe. The Indians had agreed to a boundary "the distance a man could walk in a day and a half." The colonists had hired three men who ran instead of walked. After Thomson resolved the problem, the Delaware adopted him into their tribe and gave him a name that in their language meant "the Man Who Tells the Truth."

Thomson's name fit him well as he became a leader in the colonists' protests against unfair British regulations and taxes. He often worked behind the scenes to rally Americans to fight for independence. **John Adams** referred to him as "the soul of truth and honor." He traveled throughout the country, gathering supporters of independence, while listening to objectors who did not want to go to war. When people saw him coming, they would say, "Here comes Thomson, here comes the truth."

Thomson was a widower without children when he married Hannah Harrison in 1774. He was operating a successful business as a rum maker in Philadelphia when he learned that the Continental Congress had unanimously chosen him as its secretary. He began keeping detailed notes that included every accusation, threat, and incidence of near-physical violence that erupted among the delegates (representatives), who often disagreed.

On July 4, 1776, after the congress finally voted to declare independence from Britain, only two people signed the first copy of the **Declaration of Independence—John Hancock** as president of the congress, and Charles Thomson as secretary. Thomson arranged for John Dunlap to print fifty copies of the document with the two names, and he distributed them to the other delegates. By August 2, 1776, one copy had the signatures of fifty-six delegates. This was the copy of the Declaration of Independence printed by **Mary Katherine Goddard** in the Boston newspaper the following January.

Thomson was in charge of the spies the congress employed both in America and overseas. He was the messenger sent to inform **George Washington** that the congress had elected him the first president of the United States. When the nation needed an official seal to mark its documents and papers, Thomson was responsible for settling the disputes among Franklin, Adams, and Jefferson. In fact, Thomson himself created the final design for the seal. He placed an image of a bald eagle in the center, saying the new nation was "on the wing and rising." He gave the eagle a shield on its breast, but he put no supports on either side. He said this was "to denote

The Great Seal of the United States, designed by Charles Thomson, is used to identify official U.S. documents and papers.

that the United States of America ought to rely on its own virtue." He drew the eagle holding an olive branch in its right talon and a cluster of thirteen arrows in the other to show "the power of peace and war." The eagle's beak held a banner with the country's first motto, *E Pluribus Unum*, Latin for "Out of Many, One."

Above the eagle's head Thomson drew a golden glory breaking through a cloud and surrounding thirteen stars, a silver constellation on an azure field. The official die (mold) of the Great Seal is technically incorrect because the die maker failed to show the light "breaking through a cloud" as Thomson designed it.

Thomson presented his design to Congress on June 20, 1782. It was unanimously approved as the Great Seal of the United States of America that same day.

In 1785 Thomson helped found the Philadelphia Society for Promoting Agriculture. The organization still exists and is the oldest continuing agricultural organization in the country. Thomson was a dedicated beekeeper and experimented with new agricultural techniques and crop production.

Thomson completed his last official act on July 25, 1789, by delivering all official papers and records of the Confederation of States to the new U.S. government. He did not, however, deliver his personal volumes of notes, because he planned to write a book about the history of the revolution. Before writing that history, Thomson completed a translation of the Bible that he had started working on long before his retirement from public service. In 1808 his translation from the Greek texts were the first to be published in North America. Copies of the Thomson Bible still exist today.

Thomson authored other works, but the most patriotic book he wrote may be the one he never published. Before his death, the man of truth carefully destroyed each page of his account of what happened in America's struggle to win independence. When friends asked why he did not publish the manuscript, he simply said, "I ought not."

Thomson died on August 16, 1824. He is buried in Laurel Hill Cemetery in Philadelphia.

BARON FRIEDRICH VON STEUBEN

PRUSSIAN VOLUNTEER WHO TRAINED AMERICA TO FIGHT
1730–1794

Platoons! To the right, wheel! Forward march!

—Baron Friedrich von Steuben,
training American soldiers at Valley Forge

Not all extraordinary patriots were Americans. Friedrich Wilhelm Ludolf Gerhard Augustin von Steuben was a Prussian baron who volunteered to fight for America in the Revolution because he believed in America's right to be independent. The methods he used for training soldiers in battle and in peace are still used by military leaders in many countries.

Steuben was born in Magdeburg, Prussia (now Germany). His father was an engineer in the military. Steuben became an officer in the Prussian military by the age of seventeen. His ability as an officer resulted in his promotion to the general staff serving at Frederick the Great's headquarters. The training and experience he received there proved tremendously valuable when he later served under General **George Washington** in the American Revolution.

Steuben left the Prussian army in 1763 at the age of thirty-three. He went to work for one of the small German states, where he received the title of baron.

In 1777 Steuben went to Paris seeking loans to help the German prince for whom he worked. While in Paris, Steuben learned that **Benjamin Franklin** was also there. Steuben applied to him for work in the Continental army in America. Franklin wrote a letter to Washington introducing Steuben as "Lieutenant General in the King of Prussia's service."

Steuben arrived at Portsmouth, New Hampshire, on September 26, 1777, more than a year after the colonies had declared independence from Britain. He joined the army as a volunteer without pay and began service at Valley Forge, Pennsylvania. He did not speak English at that time and communicated through Washington's French-speaking aides, including **Alexander Hamilton** and **Nathanael Greene**. They assisted Steuben in drafting strategy and training plans for the American soldiers, whom someone described to him as "more of a mob than an army."

Steuben began training the Americans by creating a "model company." He assembled and trained a group of one hundred soldiers, and then he sent each man to train another company of one hundred soldiers.

Washington's army had experienced some success prior to Steuben's formal training. Its guerrilla (irregular) tactics sometimes gave them an advantage when the soldiers confronted formal lines of British troops, whose red coats made a bright target. Prior to Steuben's arrival, however, most new soldiers were placed into units without any training and were easily defeated by the British "redcoats." Steuben introduced a system of progressive training, similar to present-day methods: Drill instructors trained new soldiers first without weapons, then pro-

Baron Friedrich von Steuben trained American soldiers in the art of efficient combat on the battlefield.

gressed to training with weapons, then followed with advanced training. Only then were the soldiers sent into battle. Steuben's tactics brought order and discipline to the troops, making them more efficient in the confusion of combat.

Steuben emphasized the need to fire rifles quickly on the battlefield. He drilled men in the handling of firearms until the sequence of loading and firing became quick, methodical motions. Firing the rifles of that era required eight counts and fifteen motions. Rifles had to be reloaded with both powder and shot after each firing. Establishing an efficient sequence of motions to reload and fire in battle immediately helped decrease fatalities among the Americans.

Next Steuben tackled camp cleanliness. During the winter of 1777–1778, more than 2,500 men died of the contagious diseases typhus and dysentery because of the unsanitary conditions in the camps and the lack of supplies. Military camps had no organized layout of tents and huts. There were no standardized methods for handling or storing supplies. There were no designated areas for human waste. Dead animals were left to rot where they lay. Steuben's plan laid out rows of tents for commanders and other rows for officers and enlisted soldiers. Streets were laid through the camp. Kitchen areas were located on the uphill side of the camp, and outdoor latrines (toilets used by a large number of people) were located on the opposite, downhill side.

Steuben's methods proved to be tremendously successful. The battle for Monmouth, New Jersey, in June, 1778, ended in a draw. Thanks to their training, the Americans held their own against the redcoats. Washington recommended that Steuben be appointed an inspector general of the Continental army, and Congress approved the appointment.

Steuben despised traitors. One event often told by military historians clearly showed his disgust for Benedict Arnold, an American who deserted his post at West Point, New York, and aided the British. During an inspection Steuben learned there was a soldier in the regiment named Arnold, and he ordered him to step forward.

"Change your name, brother-soldier; you are too respectable to bear the name of a traitor," he told the soldier.

"What name shall I take, General?"

"Take any other name; mine is at your service," Steuben replied. The soldier accepted his offer and had his last name changed on the regiment roll to Steuben, never using the name *Arnold* again.

During the winter of 1778–1779, Steuben finished writing *Regulations for the Order and Discipline of the Troops of the United States*, also known as the Blue Book. It gave the details of the training plan he established at Valley Forge. This information is still used in modern military operations. When the War of Independence ended in 1783, Steuben prepared defense plans for the new nation, believing America needed to maintain a strong defense and always be prepared to fight any attacker.

Baron von Steuben settled in New York on land granted to him for his service to the country. He died in 1794 without heirs and left his property to Benjamin Walker and William North, two of his aides.

BENJAMIN EDES

VOICE OF THE SONS OF LIBERTY
1732–1803

The colonists believe they are fully capable of managing their own affairs.

—Benjamin Edes, editor,
Boston Gazette and Country Journal, 1764

Benjamin Edes knew that when the latest edition of his *Boston Gazette and Country Journal* newspaper reached the British soldiers in Boston, his business and even his life would be in danger. Edes had boldly printed **Patrick Henry**'s rebellious resolutions (strong statements) opposing the Stamp Act. Introduced in 1765, the Stamp Act required the American colonists to pay British officials to place stamps on all official documents, such as deeds and contracts. Many newspaper editors in the colonies were afraid to publish Henry's statements.

Not Edes. This was not the first time, nor would it be the last, that the daring Boston newspaper editor would fan the flames of public opinion, leading to American independence.

Benjamin Edes was born in October, 1732, to Peter and Ester Edes in Charlestown, Massachusetts. At age twenty-two Edes and a partner, John Gill, founded *The Boston Gazette and Country Journal*. Gill later left to publish another newspaper. Edes also published *The North-American Almanack*, which included articles about life in New England. **Paul Revere** drew illustrations for both the *Almanack* and the *Gazette*.

Many of Edes's columns and editorials expressed anger at the British government. He made no effort to present the British viewpoint that their laws and taxes were justified because of the money they were spending to help the colonists in America.

Edes's willingness to publish and distribute protests against the Stamp Act quickly aroused the anger of the colonists about the new British law. The Americans argued that the act was illegal because the colonies did not have a vote in England's Parliament (legislature). These protests resulted in the slogan "No taxation without representation!"

The British repealed (canceled) the Stamp Act in 1766. Edes saw the repeal as a stunning victory in his war using words as weapons against the British. He began printing every story he could to convince the Loyalists (Americans who were loyal to British rule) to take a stand against other unfair laws.

On March 12, 1770, Edes was outraged by what has come to be known as the Boston Massacre. Some young men in Boston confronted a British soldier in an alley. The soldier slashed two of the men with his sword in the confrontation.

A crowd of local people chased the soldier to his barracks. Edes described in the *Gazette* what happened next: "In less than a minute, ten or twelve soldiers rushed from the barracks with cutlasses [small swords] drawn."

The soldiers pushed the crowd back, injuring several with their swords. The angry crowd then attacked the soldiers with snowballs. The *Gazette* story continues, "The captain commanded the soldiers to fire their muskets . . ."

When the fight ended, the *Gazette* account listed three in the crowd of local people as dead: **Crispus Attucks**, an African American, was the first to die; Samuel Gray and James Caldwell were next. Two others died later. Edes's report of the event convinced a number of young men to join the opposition to the British rule in the Colonies.

Edes not only wrote about others who were actively defying British laws, he also participated in antitaxation activities as a member of the Sons of Liberty, a secret organization of mostly young men who actively opposed the British forcing taxes on the colonists. Edes took part in one of the most memorable acts of the Sons of Liberty. On the afternoon of December 16, 1773, members gathered at Edes's house. There they disguised themselves as Indians and headed for Boston Harbor. **Samuel Adams**, the leader of the Sons of Liberty, directed them to board British ships filled with tea. They overpowered the ships' crews and dumped the tea into Boston Harbor to protest the British tax on tea. The surprise raid became known as the Boston Tea Party.

"Many persons wish that there were as many dead bodies floating in the harbor as there were chests of tea," **John Adams** said when he described the raid. Adams was an American patriot and a lawyer who had previously defended the British soldiers responsible for the Boston Massacre.

Edes had been appointed the official printer for the colonial government in Massachusetts, but because of his participation in the Boston Tea Party, he lost this business. He barely escaped to Watertown, Massachusetts, when the British besieged Boston during 1774 and 1775, invading homes, destroying property, and stopping supplies from coming into Boston as punishment for the Boston Tea Party. This did not stop the growing rebellion, however. It had the opposite effect, inspiring the colonists to increase their resistance to the British.

The United States of America was an independent nation when Benjamin Edes discontinued publication of the *Gazette* in 1798. He died in 1803. Newspapers throughout the country praised him for his fearless determination to see America free from British rule. They reported that "the voice of liberty" had been silenced, but the vision of liberty that Edes inspired, both in words and deeds, would never die.

RICHARD HENRY LEE

WRITER OF RESOLUTIONS FOR
REVOLUTION
1732–1794

Resolved: that these United Colonies are, and of right ought to be, free and independent States . . .

—Richard Henry Lee,
in his resolution presented June 7, 1776,
to the Continental Congress

Richard Henry Lee looked at the men of Virginia's Westmoreland County gathered before him on February 27, 1766. Among the 115 patriots were three of Lee's brothers and the four brothers of **George Washington**.

"We will exert every faculty to prevent the execution of the Stamp Act in any instance whatsoever in this Colony," Lee read from the document he had written. A cheer arose as the men eagerly signed their names to Lee's resolution protesting Britain's newest tax on the colonists. Ten years later Lee would stand before another group of men, this time in Philadelphia, to read another resolution. That resolution would declare America's independence.

Richard Henry Lee was born in Westmoreland County, Virginia, on January 20, 1732. He was one of six sons and two daughters born to the prominent Virginia planter Thomas Lee and his wife, Hannah. Thomas Lee owned more than sixteen thousand acres in Virginia and Maryland, where he built a large house known as Stratford Hall. His father's wealth made it possible for Richard to go to school in Yorkshire, England, where he developed a love for science and literature. His classmates considered him shy, and even after he returned to America, he was described as "the quiet one" of his family.

Richard married Ann Aylett in 1757, and they had four children. After her death he married Anne Gaskins Pinchard. They had five children.

Lee became friends with **Patrick Henry** while serving in the Virginia House of Burgesses (Representatives). In 1758 Lee made a passionate speech proposing that America stop importing slaves, although he was a slaveholder. His bold efforts failed, but his superbly spoken, fiery protest against slavery forever changed his public image.

Lee was among those who suggested organizing, and was later a member of, the Virginia Committee of Correspondence. Committees of correspondence in the colonies were organized to promote resistance to British political and economic pressures. Lee believed the colonies had to be united if they were going to be free.

Lee became a strong and vocal opponent of the Stamp Act of 1765, which required colonists to pay for an official British stamp on each piece of paper used by the colonists, such as legal documents, licenses, and even newspapers. The British felt these taxes were justified because of the money they had spent defending the colonists during the French and Indian War (1754–1763), when the British had helped the colonists resist the attacks of the French and their Indian allies. Lee's Westmoreland Resolution against the Stamp Act, which he read to the men at Westmoreland in 1766, threatened "danger and disgrace" to anyone who paid the tax. The colonists formed an association with a list of items ranging from gloves to gold rings that they agreed not to order from Britain until the Stamp Act was withdrawn. Their efforts worked. The Stamp Act was repealed in 1766.

Lee was now described as a "born orator" with a "fine polish of language" that he used "like a flame" to excite the colonists to oppose British rule. By 1774 the sentiment for independence had reached such a level that a call for unity among the thirteen colonies resulted in the First Continental Congress. Lee was one of the delegates from Virginia who attended the Congress in Philadelphia. Before the meeting he had injured his hand in a hunting accident and he kept it wrapped in black silk. He used his wrapped hand "like a conductor's baton" each time he spoke for the rights of the colonists.

The Second Continental Congress was held in 1775 and 1776. Richard Henry and his brother, Francis Lightfoot Lee, were delegates to this congress. The Lees had become a leading family of American patriots. Another of the brothers, Thomas Ludwell Lee, helped write Virginia's resolutions demanding independence. Two other brothers, William and Arthur, went to England and sought support for the American Revolution. They also provided valuable information to Richard Henry and Francis Lightfoot about the plans of the British to stop America from becoming an independent nation. The Lees became close friends with **John Adams** and John's cousin, **Samuel Adams**, and their friendships helped unite the northern and southern colonies.

Richard Henry Lee helped write the Declaration of Rights of the Colonies. After months of secret debates and arguments in Philadelphia, he presented the bill, which authorized the **Declaration of Independence** to Congress. The actual declaration, written by **Thomas Jefferson** with assistance from John Adams, **Benjamin Franklin**, Robert R. Livingston, and **Roger Sherman**, was passed on July 2, 1776. Richard Henry Lee and Francis Lightfoot Lee were the only two brothers to sign the document that dissolved all ties with the British government.

In 1778 Lee signed the Articles of Confederation, the document that governed the new American nation from 1781 to 1789; however, when some of his fellow patriots wanted a constitution to replace the Articles of Confederation, Lee told them he wanted no part of it. A constitution is a set of rules and laws that tells how a government is organized and run. Lee, like other anti-Federalists, believed a constitution would create a strong central government and take away from the rights of the states and individuals.

After the states ratified (accepted) the **Constitution of the United States of America**, Lee accepted appointment as one of the first senators from Virginia. He committed himself to righting the things he felt were wrong with the Constitution and to helping create the Bill of Rights, the first ten amendments to the Constitution, which define the rights of individual citizens.

Lee died on June 19, 1794, at Chantilly, his Virginia estate.

FRANCIS MARION

THE SWAMP FOX
1732–1795

He lived without fear, and died without reproach.

—Francis Marion's tombstone

Francis Marion could hear his brothers calling for him, but he did not move. He was half the size of other ten-year-old boys, who often teased him for being so small. Francis didn't care. He could hide so well in the forests and swamps near his family's farm that no one, not even his brothers, could ever find him.

Francis Marion was born in 1732 in St. John's Parish, in the American colony of South Carolina. His parents were Gabriel and Esther Cordes Marion. He had two sisters and four older brothers. He was often sick as a baby, but he became strong and smart while playing in the swamp along the Santee River, where he learned to hunt and to catch fish and turtles to eat. The swamp was the only school he ever attended—instead of books, he studied the skills of the Indians who had lived in the area for many years.

Against his parents' wishes when he was fifteen, Marion sailed on a ship bound for the West Indies in search of adventure. The ship never made it to the West Indies. It sank in the open seas, leaving Marion adrift in a small lifeboat for a week until it ran aground. Even though he had grown up by a river and in the swamps, he did not know how to swim!

Marion eventually returned to South Carolina to farm. When the Cherokee Indians began attacking settlers in territory the Cherokee believed belonged to them, Marion joined the militia (citizen soldiers). His horseback-riding and marksman skills, plus his knowledge of the swamps, earned him the respect of the settlers, who voted him to be their delegate (representative) to the South Carolina Provincial Congress in 1775. This congress, made up of colonists who opposed British rule in America, authorized the formation of two groups of soldiers to fight the British. Marion was made the captain of the Second Regiment.

At this time more than half of the colonists living in South Carolina were Loyalists who did not want to separate from the British. Marion taught the men who did want independence how to attack British soldiers at night and then disappear into the waterways, forests, and boggy swamps.

Marion was promoted to the rank of lieutenant colonel when the Continental army took over the state's regiments. However, thousands of British troops over-whelmed the Continental soldiers and captured the city of Charleston in 1780, making it their headquarters under the direction of the British commander

Banastre Tarleton, who ordered his troops to burn the homes and crops and to kill anyone they believed to have helped the Americans.

When the Continental army pulled out of South Carolina, Marion stayed. He formed a unit of about 150 soldiers who became known as Marion's Brigade. Though poorly equipped, with little ammunition and no pay, the men continued to harass the British severely by capturing soldiers, supplies, and communications. Tarleton called Marion "that wily ol' swamp fox" because Marion could strike without warning, then escape and disappear into the swamps where the British could not follow. Tarleton's soldiers were warned to be on the lookout for a "thin, slight fellow with a long, hawklike nose" who roamed the swamps around the Pee Dee River. Unknown to Tarleton, Marion's hideout was Snow's Island, near where the Pee Dee and Lynches rivers came together.

By keeping the British distracted, Marion and his ragged group of soldiers helped turn the tide in favor of the Americans in the south. In 1781 he joined forces with General **Nathanael Greene** of the Continental army, who had returned to South Carolina and fought in the battles of Kings Mountain, Cowpens, Guilford Courthouse, and Georgetown. With Greene, Marion and his soldiers won the Battle of Eutaw Springs on September 8, 1781, forcing the British to retreat to North Carolina.

That same year while he was still serving as a soldier, Marion was elected to the South Carolina Senate. He was reelected in 1782. After the war Marion trained troops at Fort Johnson, South Carolina, and wrote the first American military book explaining the unusual fighting methods he developed, which are now known as guerrilla warfare. "The page of history never furnished his equal," Greene said.

Marion married Mary Esther Videau in 1786. They had no children. He died on February 27, 1795, at the home he called Pond Bluff, and is buried at Belle Isle, near present-day St. Stephens, South Carolina.

While Marion is best remembered as the daring Swamp Fox who refused to give up the fight for independence, and is recognized as "the father of military special forces," he is also remembered for his belief in the importance of public education to instill patriotism in future generations.

"Men will always fight for their government, according to their sense of its value. To value it aright, they must understand it. This they cannot do without education," he said. Frances Marion University in Florence, South Carolina, is named in his honor.

GEORGE WASHINGTON

THE FATHER OF OUR COUNTRY
1732–1799

Cherish the Union.

—President George Washington

Crowds watched as George Washington stepped to the balcony of New York City's Federal Hall, then the capitol building of the United States. The tall outdoorsman wore a dark brown suit with silver buttons, white stockings, and black shoes with silver buckles. His hair was carefully powdered in the custom of an American gentleman in his fifty-eighth year. Washington raised his right hand and placed his left hand on an open Bible. A minute later he was no longer the commander in chief who had led the Continental army to victory in the Revolutionary War. On April 30, 1789, George Washington became the first president of the United States of America.

George Washington was born on February 22, 1732, in Westmoreland County, Virginia. His father was a widower with three children when he married Mary Ball. George was the oldest of their five children. His early classrooms were primarily the rivers, forests, and fields of the family farm on Pope's Creek along the Potomac River, though he was taught reading, mathematics, surveying (determining land boundaries), and good manners at home. His father died when George was eleven, and at sixteen George went to live with his half-brother, Lawrence, at Mount Vernon, Virginia. He never attended college, a regret he expressed later in his life.

By age sixteen Washington was a surveyor helping to map the Shenandoah lands of Virginia. In 1751 George accompanied Lawrence on a trip to Barbados, West Indies, where George caught smallpox. The disease left his face scarred for the rest of his life. George later inherited Mount Vernon.

Washington served in the British army for six years and fought in the French and Indian War (1754–1763), during which the British fought the French and the Indians for control of the Ohio Valley. It was Washington's attacks in 1754 on a French scouting party that ignited the war, bringing him much criticism. During one fierce battle with the Indians, who had sided with France, the six-foot, two-inch-tall Washington was the only red-coated British officer on horseback who was not killed.

"I had four bullets through my coat and two horses shot from under me, yet escaped unhurt," Washington wrote to his brother, John. Years later one of the leaders of the Indians came to visit Washington and told him, "I have come to honor the man who is the particular favorite of Heaven, who can never die in battle."

Washington was not happy as a British soldier, so he resigned to return to Mount Vernon, where he planned to spend the rest of his life as a farmer. In 1759 he married Martha Dandridge Custis, a widow with two young children.

Washington entered politics as a member of the Virginia House of Burgesses (representatives) in 1758, and he served until 1774. In 1775 Washington learned that the British were not going to honor his claims for land he had surveyed, as they had promised. He led the colonists to form the Continental Congress to oppose the British government, and during the winter of 1774–1775, he gathered a militia (citizen soldiers) in Virginia. Congress created the Continental army to defend the colonists, and on June 15, 1775, it unanimously elected Washington as general and commander in chief.

Washington led the Continental army from 1775 to 1782 and also created a navy. During those grueling years he was often on the battlefields but was never seriously wounded. He suffered tremendous financial losses and endured bitter cold, frequent hunger, and other hardships, leading the thirteen colonies in a war they were not prepared to fight. He later said his greatest accomplishments were keeping his soldiers paid and refusing to lose his quick temper.

King George III of Britain branded Washington guilty of treason. Friends and foes alike described Washington as courageous, quiet, stern, disciplined, steady in the face of danger, brilliant, and absolutely devoted to the United States of America. His crossing of the Delaware River on Christmas night, 1776, to attack the enemy has become a symbol of the heroism of the Revolutionary War.

The British general Charles Cornwallis surrendered at Yorktown, New York, on October 19, 1781, and a weary Washington retired from the army. He did not retire from serving his country, though. He believed that the Articles of Confederation that governed the United States were too weak to serve the needs of the new nation. Under the articles Congress could not collect taxes, raise a military force, or pay money it owed. In May 1787 the Constitutional Convention met in Philadelphia and began writing a constitution (a set of rules and laws that tells how a government is organized and run). Washington was the first president of the convention. He wanted to ensure that the **Constitution of the United States of America** prevented any person or group from having total control of the government.

When the Constitution was ratified (accepted), Congress knew there was no one more qualified than Washington to be the nation's first president. **Charles Thomson** carried to Washington at Mount Vernon the letter that told him he had been elected unanimously. **Henry Knox**, who had served as one of Washington's battlefield generals, encouraged him to accept the job and become "the father of our country." Reluctantly, Washington accepted. He made it clear that he would be a president of the people, not the king of an empire. **John Adams** was elected vice president.

Washington, like many other large landholders in colonial America, owned many slaves. Although he became convinced slavery was unjust and immoral, he did not support the abolition (elimination) of slavery while in office, fearing the issue would split apart the young republic. He wrote, "I clearly foresee that nothing but the rooting out of slavery can perpetuate the existence of our [federal] union."

Washington was reelected in 1792. His favorite meals as president included cream of peanut soup, mashed sweet potatoes with coconut, and string beans with mushrooms. These reflect that he had lost all his natural teeth at an early age. Contrary to myth, his false teeth were made of ivory, not wood.

Washington could have run for a third term as president in 1796, but he did not. He was tired and distressed that his friends **Thomas Jefferson** and **Alexander Hamilton** were leading the country in two competing political directions.

Washington's letters written as commander in chief of the army played an important part in winning independence. He wrote almost every day to praise, instruct, and encourage his soldiers and to promote the cause of America's freedom. While hundreds of Washington's military letters and papers have been published, only three of the many letters that Washington and Martha wrote to each other exist. Late in life she burned their personal correspondence to protect the private life the Washingtons had shared during forty years of marriage. The Washingtons had no children, but George did have hunting dogs that he treated like family. He gave them such names as Sweet Lips and True Love.

Washington was pleased but embarrassed that the nation's new capital had been named for him. He sometimes rode his horse around Washington, D.C., to watch the construction of the new city. On December 12, 1799, Washington went horseback riding at Mount Vernon and developed a sore throat. Doctors tried the usual treatments of the time, including bleeding him to get rid of any poisons, and had him drink molasses, vinegar, and melted butter. Of course, these treatments could not stop the infection. He died on December 14, 1799. Martha died less than three years later on May 22, 1802. They are buried at Mount Vernon. In his will Washington directed that his slaves be freed upon his death, which was extremely unusual during this period in America.

George Washington has been honored in countless ways. Streets, cities, parks, and buildings around the world have been named for him. In 1847 he became the first president whose likeness appeared on a U.S. postage stamp. His face on the dollar bill and the quarter is recognized around the world. Millions of visitors come each year to see the Washington Monument in Washington, D.C. Probably no honor would have pleased Washington more, however, than the one bestowed upon him in 1976: He was appointed General of the Armies, and a presidential decree confirmed that he could never be outranked by another U.S. military officer.

ROBERT MORRIS

THE MAN WHO FINANCED THE REVOLUTION
1734–1806

He was a friend to be sought and a foe to be feared.

—Ellis Paxson Oberholtzer, Biographer

Robert Morris sat in the Philadelphia jail where he had been imprisoned for the past three years. His crime? He had signed the **Declaration of Independence** and then taken on the task of raising the money to pay for the Revolutionary War, using every penny he had and borrowing every penny he could. Now, in 1801, the United

States of America was a free country, but he was no longer a free man because he could not pay his debts.

Morris was born in Liverpool, England, on January 31, 1734. He came to the American colonies with his father when he was thirteen and was apprenticed to a countinghouse, or trading firm, in Philadelphia. An apprentice learned a trade by working with someone who was already skilled. By 1754 he was a partner in the firm and had become extremely wealthy bringing goods into the colonies from all over the world with his company's fleet of ships.

In 1765 Britain placed a tax on the colonies called the Stamp Act. The act required colonists to buy tax stamps to place on all legal documents, such as deeds and contracts. Morris joined other colonists in opposing the act. The Stamp Act protests spread throughout the colonies as men such as the lawyer **Patrick Henry** and the newspaper editor **Benjamin Edes** argued that the act was illegal because the colonies were not represented in Parliament (Britain's legislature).

Morris agreed to support Henry's "Non-importation Resolutions" even though he knew it would severely hurt his trading business. These resolutions urged Americans to stop importing goods from Britain until the Stamp Act was repealed. The Stamp Act was repealed in 1766, but this did not put an end to the growing conflicts between Britain and the colonies.

In 1769 Morris married twenty-year-old Mary White. Six years later the first shots of the Revolution were fired at Lexington and Concord, Massachusetts, between colonists and British soldiers. The Continental Congress appealed to Morris's firm to import secretly guns and ammunition for the war. Two months later Morris was selected to be a Pennsylvania delegate to the Continental Congress, but he did not support independence at that point and was absent when the Declaration of Independence was signed on July 2, 1776. One month later he changed his mind and added his signature.

"I think it is the duty of a good citizen to follow when he cannot lead," Morris said.

Some believed he signed the declaration in hopes of profiting in some way; however, from that day on Morris supported independence and played a crucial role in raising money for the financially-strapped country. When Congress issued paper money called "continentals," he warned that "the Continental currency keeps losing its credit. Many people refuse to receive it." Soon the phrase "I don't give a continental" became a way of saying that something was worthless.

Morris obtained loans for General **George Washington** to feed, clothe, and pay his troops and buy supplies. Washington once was so desperate to keep his troops from deserting that he promised his soldiers a ten-dollar bonus if they would stay and fight. He told Morris he didn't know how he could keep the promise. Morris borrowed fifty thousand dollars from a Quaker merchant, pledging only his honor for security.

Without Morris's help, General **Nathanael Greene** would not have had the weapons to win the important battles of 1780. The next year Morris helped organize the Bank of North America for the purpose of lending money to the Continental Congress. The bank gathered $400,000 from investors.

As the Revolution wore on, the financial situation worsened. When eighty armed American soldiers came to his office demanding back pay, Morris fled to the home of a friend to hide. Congress passed controls and laws requiring merchants to accept the continentals, but this only made the problem worse. Inflation (runaway price increases) made the paper money good for nothing more than wallpaper.

When the French general **Marquis de Lafayette** urged General Washington to move his army to Yorktown, New York, in 1781 because the British were there, Washington had no funds to pay or feed the troops. Morris convinced citizens of the colonies along the route—New Jersey, Delaware, Maryland, and Virginia—to provide supplies as the army marched through.

Nonetheless, the army still needed money to buy equipment. Morris knew that the French had already advanced large sums of money to the Americans, but in an act of desperation he pleaded with the commander of the French troops in America to divert a huge shipment of silver, which had arrived by ship to purchase supplies for the French, to be sent instead to General Washington. The silver reached Washington just in time for him to equip and position his troops. Washington's army then achieved a stunning victory at Yorktown, forcing the British general Charles Cornwallis to surrender on October 19, 1781.

After the war Morris returned to his shipping business and opened trade with China. Though he was no longer wealthy, his skill at raising money was still admired. The Pennsylvania Assembly named him a delegate to the Constitutional Convention of 1787, where he supported ratification (acceptance) of the new **Constitution of the United States of America**. After the Constitution was ratified in 1788, he served as a senator from Pennsylvania. He declined Washington's offer of becoming secretary of the treasury in 1789.

Morris later invested in land, hoping to help develop farms and towns in the new nation. The investments were a failure. Unable to pay his debts, he was sentenced to prison in 1798, where he remained until 1801.

Morris was freed after Congress passed a national bankruptcy law that prevented people from being kept in prison for failure to pay their debts; however, he had no way to start a new business and few friends left. He died a poor and broken-hearted patriot on May 7, 1806.

JOHN ADAMS

PRESERVER OF LIBERTY
1735–1826

It is extremely difficult to preserve liberty.

—John Adams

John Adams eagerly unfolded the letter from his wife that the post rider had just delivered. What he read made his heart pound: Abigail Adams had witnessed a battle near their home in Massachusetts between American colonists and British soldiers. He carefully folded the paper. He would reply later. Now he must hurry and share this startling news with the other delegates meeting in Philadelphia to unite the colonists against British rule.

John Adams was born on October 19, 1735, in Braintree (now Quincy), Massachusetts, on farmland that had been owned by his family for several generations. He was the oldest son of John and Susanna Boylston Adams. There were a number of doctors in his mother's family, but John did not want a career in medicine.

At the age of sixteen, Adams entered Harvard College, where Latin, history, and philosophy were his favorite subjects. Upon graduating he began to teach; later, he studied law. Adams loved to learn as much as he could about a subject, and even after he became a well-known lawyer, he often identified himself as a "student."

Adams married Abigail Smith in 1764. They had five children, including John Quincy Adams, who would become the sixth president of the United States. The year after John and Abigail married, Britain passed the Stamp Act, which especially angered the colonists. The Stamp Act required colonists to buy stamps to affix to all legal documents, such as deeds and contracts, and other pieces of paper. Adams wrote a resolution (strong statement) protesting the act. Although no methods for making or sending copies of the handwritten document existed, the words Adams wrote spread like wildfire. He expressed the idea of "no taxation without representation," because the colonists did not have a say in the British government.

Adams moved his law practice to Boston in 1768 as the colonists began moving toward independence. More important to him than independence were the rights of individuals to be protected by the law. An incident that occurred in 1770 that became known as the Boston Massacre proved Adams's dedication to this belief. One evening a man named **Crispus Attucks** and others in a crowd of angry colonists threw snowballs at British soldiers. The soldiers fired into the crowd, and five of the colonists were killed. Adams was asked to defend the soldiers. He did, winning the case for the soldiers without losing his reputation as a supporter of the colonists.

When the First Continental Congress met in September 1774, Adams attended as a delegate from Massachusetts. Adams still did not want the colonies to break away from Britain, but he knew war was coming and that the colonies must prepare.

At the Second Continental Congress, in May, 1775, Adams insisted that the congress set up an independent government and raise an army. He nominated Colonel **George Washington** to be the Continental army's commander in chief. He wrote a letter to Abigail telling her that on June 7, 1776, **Richard Henry Lee** proposed "that these United Colonies are, and of right ought to be, free and independent states."

Adams was one of the five men the congress assigned to write the formal **Declaration of Independence**. He and the youngest delegate, **Thomas Jefferson**, worked closely for several days to produce the document that has since become known as the birth certificate of the United States of America.

Adams's wit and wisdom made him the ideal person to seek support for America in Europe during the Revolutionary War. He wrote many funny stories in his diary about his experiences with **Benjamin Franklin** in France, where they sought assistance against the British. Adams not only signed the Declaration of Independence, but he also signed the Treaty of Peace with Britain after the war.

The **Constitution of the United States of America**, adopted in 1789, provided a set of rules and laws for how the U.S. government was to be organized and run. At that time the presidential candidate with the most votes became president. The candidate with the second-most votes became vice president. George Washington was elected the first president of the United States, and John Adams was its first vice president.

In the election of 1796, Adams was elected president, and Thomas Jefferson was elected vice president. By now political parties with opposing views had formed in the United States. Adams's political party was the Federalists, and Jefferson's party was the Democratic-Republicans. Having the president and the vice president from opposing political parties created great conflict.

Adams was certain he would win the presidential election of 1800 as the Federalist candidate; to his surprise the leaders of his own party, including Alexander Hamilton, turned against him and supported another Federalist candidate, Charles Cotesworth Pinckney. Both Adams and Pinckney were defeated when Democratic-Republican candidates Thomas Jefferson and Aaron Burr tied with seventy-three electoral votes each. The election had to be decided in the House of Representatives, with the vote going to Jefferson.

Adams was so bitter about losing that he moved to his farm in Massachusetts and never participated in public affairs again. He did, however, live to see his son, John Quincy Adams, elected president. The son of a president being elected president did not happen again in the United States until the election of President George W. Bush in 2000.

John and Abigail were married for fifty-four years. She greatly influenced him. In 1812 she helped her husband overcome his differences with Jefferson by encouraging Adams to write Jefferson a letter explaining his feelings and asking Jefferson to write him back to explain his. Adams did as she suggested. After writing the letter, he sprinkled sand on the wet ink and then blew the sand away, as was the custom to ensure that the ink did not smear. "It was as if I had blown away twelve years of sadness in those grains of sand," he told Abigail. She died in 1818.

Adams and Jefferson continued to write long letters to each other. Many of their letters included their memories of their youth, when they worked together for America's independence. Adams died at his farm in Massachusetts on July 4, 1826. That date marked the fiftieth anniversary of the signing of the Declaration of Independence. Adams's last words were reported to be "Only Jefferson lives." Unknown to Adams, Jefferson had died just a few hours earlier at his home in Virginia.

PAUL REVERE

A SON OF LIBERTY WHO RODE INTO HISTORY
1735–1818

The fate of a nation was riding that night.

—Henry Wadsworth Longfellow,
"Paul Revere's Ride," 1860

Paul Revere waited impatiently as midnight approached. There, he saw it! Two lanterns were burning in the bell tower of Boston's Christ Church! Revere sprang into his saddle and rode toward Lexington, Massachusetts, stopping at every home to warn his fellow citizens that the British "regulars" were coming. Revere became famous for his ride on the night of April 18, 1775, thanks to a poem written by Henry Wadsworth Longfellow in 1860. It was not, however, Revere's only patriotic contribution to America's struggle for independence.

Revere was born on January 1, 1735, in Boston, to Apollos and Deborah Hitchbourn Rivoire. Apollos was a French immigrant who changed his name to Paul Revere shortly after arriving in America. The Reveres had at least nine children. Young Paul was the second surviving son.

Young Paul attended North Writing School. He then went to work with his father to learn the art of making things from copper, gold, and silver. His father died when he was nineteen. Paul's superb silversmithing skills supported the rest of the Revere family.

Revere married Sarah Orne in 1757. She died in 1773, shortly after giving birth to their eighth child. Revere married Rachel Walker the next year, and they had eight children.

During the 1770s Revere became part of the Sons of Liberty, a secret organization of mostly young men who harassed the British for placing what they felt were unreasonable taxes and laws on the colonists. In 1773 Revere joined **Samuel Adams**, **Benjamin Edes**, and about fifty others who dressed as Mohawk Indians and threw tea from British ships into Boston Harbor. They were protesting not only the tax on tea but also all the British laws they felt were unfair. This event, which became known as the Boston Tea Party, only brought more problems for the colonists from the British.

Revere, a talented artist with pen as well as with metal, drew political cartoons attacking the British that aroused support for independence among the colonists. He worked for the Boston Committee of Correspondence and was the principal rider carrying messages for the Massachusetts Committee of Safety to New York and Philadelphia. These committees were made up of colonists in communities who shared information about British activities with colonists in other communities.

On December 13, 1774, Revere made a ride that could have been more important than the one for which he became famous the following year. He braved the ice on the Boston Post Road to warn of a potential landing in New Hampshire of British troops under orders to take away the colonists' rifles and supplies. The weather kept the British from landing, but word of Revere's courage as a rider warning of danger circulated throughout the colonies.

Through winter and into spring, Revere and his friends, including **James Otis** and Dr. Joseph Warren, continually kept track of British troops' movements. Revere arranged with another member of the Sons of Liberty to create a signal in the Christ Church bell tower that would warn if the British soldiers were advancing toward Lexington and Concord. If the British were marching out of Boston on land, one lantern would burn from the bell tower. Two lanterns meant the British were traveling by water.

While visiting with a friend at a tavern, Dr. Warren overheard plans for a British mission to arrest **John Hancock** and **Samuel Adams**, who were known for their anti-British activities with the Sons of Liberty. On April 18, 1775, Warren sent for Revere and told him to ride to Lexington, where Hancock and Adams were hiding in the home of a parson (clergyman), to warn them to escape.

Two friends rowed Revere from Boston to Charlestown. There he borrowed a horse and, under a bright moon, began his ride, warning the citizens along the route that "the regulars" were coming to take away their guns. William Dawes and Dr. Samuel Prescott joined with Revere to ride on to Concord to warn the militia (citizen soldiers) to be ready for the British soldiers. A British patrol saw the trio and tried to capture them. Dawes was thrown from his horse and escaped on foot. Prescott managed to ride away, but Revere was taken prisoner. He quickly made up a story to frighten the soldiers, saying five hundred more colonists were coming behind him. When a shot was heard in the distance (there are various stories about where the shot came from), the patrol turned and ran.

Revere's bluff worked. Adams and Hancock got away. When seven hundred

British soldiers arrived in Lexington early on the morning of April 19, they were met in the center of the village by approximately seventy-five armed minutemen (colonists who were prepared to fight on a minute's notice). As the British surrounded the minutemen, a shot was fired. It is not clear who fired this first shot in the first battle of the American Revolution, but within moments, eight of the outnumbered minutemen were dead.

Paul Revere's engraving of the Boston Massacre

Henry Wadsworth Longfellow's epic poem "Paul Revere's Ride" presents a poetic rather than a precise picture of Revere's famous ride. Arguments such as whether Revere actually saw lantern lights in the church bell tower should not overshadow the services he rendered to America that night or after the war. Revere set up a mill in Canton, Massachusetts, to make sheets of copper so that America did not have to get its copper from England. The American navy used his copper to cover the hulls on ships.

Revere recorded the Revolutionary War in engravings, the most famous of which was his portrayal in copper of the Boston Massacre. He also produced drawings and engravings promoting the new nation, though he believed that he'd created some of his greatest works of art before the war when he had worked as a dentist, wiring in false teeth he'd carved from walrus ivory or animal teeth. He treated many American soldiers who had lost teeth during and after the war and made surgical instruments used by the Continental army's doctors.

In 1788 Revere opened a foundry to supply bolts, spikes, and nails for shipyards. The foundry also produced cannons and cast bells. Revere remained a staunch believer that the new nation needed to stay prepared with supplies and arms for future defense, and he lived to see this belief confirmed when the United States and Britain went to war again in 1812.

Revere died in 1818. A newspaper reported, "Seldom has the tomb closed upon a life so honorable and useful." He is buried in Boston's Granary Burying Ground, where John Hancock and Samuel Adams are also buried.

PATRICK HENRY

THE SON OF THUNDER
1736–1799

Give me liberty or give me death!

—Patrick Henry

Patrick Henry came to Philadelphia in May 1774 as a delegate (representative) from Virginia to the First Continental Congress. The congress, made up of representatives from twelve of the thirteen colonies, was meeting in secret to address the growing tensions with Britain. Henry was determined to unite the colonists. His opening speech before the assembly captured the hearts of listeners and established him as the greatest orator (speaker) in America: "The distinctions between Virginians, Pennsylvanians, New Yorkers, and New Englanders are no more. I am not a Virginian, but an American."

Patrick Henry was born on May 29, 1736, in Hanover County, Virginia, to John and Sarah Winston Henry. He did not like attending school, even though he was very smart. To make sure that Patrick studied and worked, his father, a tobacco farmer and surveyor, eventually educated him at home.

When he was eighteen, Henry married Sarah Shelton. His father helped him open a store with his brother, but the business soon failed, and Patrick was known as one of the laziest men in Hanover County until he decided to study law. He studied for only six weeks, easily passed the required examination, and during the next three years handled more than 1,100 cases. His superb skill in speaking before a jury became widely known. One case, known as the Parson's Cause, brought him tremendous fame because he proved that the colonists had a right to make laws governing themselves.

Henry's eloquent speaking helped him win election to the Virginia House of Burgesses (representatives) in 1765. That year the British government passed the Stamp Act, a law that required everything printed on paper to carry a government stamp that the colonists had to pay for. The Virginia colonists were furious. They turned to Henry, who joined with other colonists, including **Samuel Adams**, to fight against this law. Henry wrote seven resolutions (strong statements) against the tax and presented these resolutions to the House of Burgesses. Some of the men called Henry's words "treason" at the beginning of his speech, but by the end of the day, the men were shouting "Freedom!" Henry convinced the burgesses to pass five of the resolutions. The next day the burgesses changed their minds about one of the resolutions, but they did not change their description of Henry as "the tongue of revolution." The newspaper editor **Benjamin Edes** published Henry's resolutions, and Henry's reputation as a radical American patriot spread throughout the colonies.

When the British government repealed the Stamp Act in 1766, the colonists were even more determined to oppose other British laws they felt were unfair. After Virginia's British governor dismissed the state assembly, Henry and more than eighty other representatives immediately met and voted to join with the other colonies to form a continental congress to unite against the British. While attending the First Continental Congress, he soon became known as a firebrand (hothead or troublemaker) because of his dramatic use of words.

On March 23, 1775, Henry listened to various members of the Virginia delegation argue against revolution and in favor of making peace with Britain. He listened until he could not stand it any longer and then gave what has become known as his most famous speech. He argued that there was no way to avoid war and closed with the words that have made him immortal: "Is life so dear, or peace so sweet, as to be purchased at the price of chains and slavery? Forbid it, Almighty God! I know not what course others may take; but as for me, give me liberty or give me death!"

Henry backed up his words with action. He volunteered for the Continental army and was commissioned as a colonel in command of the First Regiment of Virginia. He did not get along with the other commanders, however, and returned in 1776 to Virginia, where he was elected governor. He served three terms as the governor.

Sarah Henry died in 1775. Two years later Patrick married Dorothea Spotswood Dandridge, a widow with a daughter. Sixteen children were born to this marriage, though not all of them lived to adulthood.

Henry strongly opposed the new **Constitution of the United States of America** and voted not to ratify (accept) it. A constitution is a set of rules and laws that tells how a government is organized and run. Henry felt the proposed constitution gave too much power to the federal government and not enough power to the states and especially endangered individual freedoms.

In 1794 Patrick and his family moved to Red Hill in Charlotte County,

Virginia. President **George Washington** asked Henry to serve as secretary of state, but he refused. He was offered an appointment as chief justice of the Supreme Court, which he also refused. He declined several other important positions because he wanted to enjoy life at Red Hill. He did agree to serve in the Virginia legislature and easily won election after a powerful speech supporting national union. One listener commented, "The Son of Thunder can still make the heavens rumble."

Patrick Henry died at Red Hill on June 6, 1799, at the age of sixty-three. He is buried at Red Hill Shrine, the family cemetery, in Charlotte County, Virginia.

JOHN HANCOCK

THE MAN WITH THE BOLD HAND
1737–1793

W e fear not death.

—John Hancock

Every man watched as thirty-nine-year-old John Hancock, president of the Second Continental Congress, stepped to the front of the room. A letter from General **George Washington** had arrived, saying that British soldiers were taking over Boston. Washington wanted permission to bombard the town in order to stop them. Wearing an elegant silk coat trimmed in gold and silver, Hancock immediately announced in a thundering voice that filled the room, "Nearly all I have in the world is in the town of Boston, but if the liberty of my country demands that they be burned to ashes, issue the order and let the cannon blaze away."

John Hancock was born on January 12, 1737, in Braintree (now Quincy), Massachusetts. His father died when John was seven. John's wealthy uncle and aunt, Thomas and Lydia Hancock, adopted and brought him to live with them in Boston. When he was eight, he entered the Boston Latin School, where classes began at 7 A.M. and lasted until 5 P.M. When he was thirteen, his uncle sent him to Harvard College, where he became friends with fellow student **John Adams**. Unlike most of the other boys in his class, Hancock did not know how to swim, but he became popular thanks to the fresh food sent by his aunt each week that he shared with his classmates.

Hancock graduated from Harvard at seventeen and went to work in his uncle's merchandise business. His honesty and dependability impressed his uncle so much that his uncle sent him to England to conduct business. When his uncle died ten years later, Hancock took control of the greatest fortune in New England. Because of his wealth most of the colonists considered him a Loyalist, a person loyal to the British king. That changed in 1764 as the British government under King George III began increasing taxes and passing laws that many colonists felt were unreasonable and unfair. **Samuel Adams**, the leader of the Sons of Liberty, knew it would be helpful to have a wealthy and knowledgeable merchant like Hancock as a member of the secret organization of Americans who opposed the British.

Adams convinced Hancock to join the Sons of Liberty and help the common people work for independence. The two men seemed an unlikely pair of friends, since Adams was neither wealthy nor highly educated. Nonetheless, they shared a commitment to freeing the colonies from British control.

In 1768 the British accused Hancock of smuggling and seized one of his cargo ships. In response a band of colonists raided the British customs (tax) office, beat the officers, and burned their boat. Soon after, Hancock played a role in the Boston Tea Party, dressing as a Mohawk Indian and throwing chests of tea off British ships into Boston Harbor.

By 1775 Hancock and Samuel Adams were at the top of the king's "most wanted" list of Americans for leading the rebellion for independence from Britain. In April of that year, a group of British soldiers was sent to find and arrest the two men. Hancock and Adams were staying in a home in Lexington, Massachusetts, when **Paul Revere**, another member of the Sons of Liberty, rode to warn them that the "regulars" (British soldiers) were coming. Hancock and Adams escaped, but the battle for independence had just begun.

Hancock was elected as a delegate (representative) from Massachusetts to the Second Continental Congress. His fellow delegates then elected him president of the congress, a position of which he was extremely proud. **Charles Thomson**, secretary of the congress, wrote that Hancock "conducted the sometimes frightful and often heated debates for and against independence with such dignity as few men could have shown."

On July 4, 1776, the Continental Congress voted to adopt the **Declaration of Independence**. Only Hancock and Thomson (as secretary) signed the first copy. Printer John Dunlap then made fifty copies, which were circulated to the rest of the delegates, who assembled to sign a fresh copy on August 2, 1776.

Hancock wrote his signature on this copy with its swirls and flourishes not to impress the king, though he told the delegates he wrote it large

John Hancock signed the Declaration of Independence in bold lettering to capture the attention of the king and impress the other delegates.

enough for the king "to see without his spectacles." The often-flamboyant Hancock wanted to impress boldly upon his fellow Americans his stand for independence. At the same time he encouraged the delegates to sign the declaration as quickly as possible because he did not want to be the only one hanged for treason!

Hancock resigned as president of Congress in 1777, but remained a member for another three years. Some believed he resigned as president because he had not been elected commander in chief of the Continental army. In fact, Hancock was not in good health. He wanted to retire from politics completely in 1780, but the citizens of Massachusetts would not hear of it. They elected him as the state's first governor. He served as governor for five years, then resigned and stayed out of politics for two years, enjoying life with his wife, Dorothy Quincy, whom he had married in 1775. Their only son died in infancy.

Massachusetts elected Hancock governor again in 1787. From late 1787 to early 1788, Governor Hancock convened 364 delegates from all across Massachusetts to consider ratifying (accepting) the **Constitution of the United States of America**. A constitution is a set of rules and laws that tells how a government is organized and run.

When it appeared that Massachusetts would not ratify the Constitution, Hancock made a speech supporting the Constitution while recommending several changes and additions. He wanted it to include a bill of rights that would protect the rights of individual citizens from a powerful central government. Samuel Adams had opposed the Constitution, but Hancock's speech changed his mind. He joined Hancock in persuading the Massachusetts delegates to ratify the Constitution in 1788.

Five years later Hancock was described as "ripe for the tomb." Thin and weakened by illness, Hancock died on October 8, 1793, in Quincy. Newspaper obituaries reported that he "calmly paid his debt to nature in the very place where he was born." He is buried in the Granary Burying Ground in Boston, where Samuel Adams and Paul Revere are also buried.

THOMAS PAINE

THE "COMMON SENSE" PATRIOT
1737–1809

Without the pen of Paine, the sword of Washington would have been wielded in vain.

—John Adams

The best-selling pamphlet published in America in 1776 was only fifty pages long and did not include the name of the author. However, *The Crisis*, written by Thomas Paine, convinced many colonists that America had a right to be an independent nation.

Thomas Paine was born in Thetford, England, on January 29, 1737. He grew up very poor. A friend described him as "always cheery and courteous, though sometimes a bit blunt." He had a very brief, basic education as a child and later had a hard time keeping jobs. His first wife died after they had been married only a year, and his second marriage ended in divorce.

In 1774 Paine met **Benjamin Franklin** in London. Franklin advised him to go to America to share his ideas and beliefs about the rights of individuals. The desire for independence was swelling by the time Paine arrived in America and became the editor of *Pennsylvania* magazine. When he wrote a pamphlet opposing slavery, Paine gained a reputation as a champion for liberty.

Less than a year after Paine arrived in America, the battles of Lexington and Concord in Massachusetts were fought between the colonists and British soldiers. Paine recognized the anger of the colonists and promoted the idea that the colonists had a right to revolt against the British government. On January 10, 1776, he began selling the first copies of his pamphlet *The Crisis*. The first sentence in the pamphlet is sometimes called the most famous opening sentence in American literature: "These are the times that try men's souls."

General **George Washington** ordered that Paine's *Crisis* pamphlet be read to his troops; teachers read it to their students; women read it while they rocked babies; and men debated it in taverns and shops throughout the colonies. More than a half-million copies were sold. In the pamphlet Paine stated that the colonies must sooner or later become independent from Britain and establish a government of the people.

"The cause of America is in a great measure the cause of all mankind," he wrote. Paine was careful to make his ideas and beliefs appealing to well-educated colonists as well as to those with little education. His reasons for supporting independence and individual rights appealed to rich and poor alike. These reasons, he wrote, were "nothing more than simple facts, plain arguments and common sense."

Paine's call for a declaration of independence helped inspire the delegates (representatives) from the colonies who met that summer at the Continental Congress. The delegates had come together to unite the colonies against British rule. Paine's influence is clearly seen in the wording of the **Declaration of Independence**. In fact, some have suggested that he wrote the first draft of the Declaration of Independence that was then edited by **Thomas Jefferson.**

Paine volunteered in the Continental army and served under General **Nathanael Greene** for a short time. He continued writing articles from a common-sense point of view after he left the military. The sixteen essays he wrote, which became known as *The Crisis Papers*, were read around the world.

In 1777 Paine was appointed secretary of the Congressional Committee on Foreign Affairs (secretary of state). This was one of the highest positions in the Revolutionary government. The American leaders often looked to him for guidance and reason in times of chaos. One story that illustrates Paine's calming influence involved a British prisoner of war named Asgill. The British had caught and killed one of General Washington's captains, so Washington decided to execute Asgill, a British soldier of equal rank. When Paine heard about Washington's plan to execute a prisoner who had nothing to do with the killing of the American captain, he sent a letter to Washington. Paine told him such an action was not justice but revenge. He reasoned with Washington to show mercy for the greater purpose of showing good judgment. Washington followed Paine's advice and did not hang Asgill.

Paine was forced to resign in 1779 because he disclosed some secret infor-mation. He served as a clerk in the Pennsylvania Assembly and continued publishing his writing for the next nine years. He used what he earned from his writing to provide supplies for American soldiers.

After America won independence, Paine returned to England, intending to focus on his ideas for building iron bridges and inventing smokeless candles. He did neither. He began publishing more books of his opinions on the rights of individuals. These writings brought charges that he was trying to overthrow the British king. He fled to France, where in 1789 he became a hero for participating in the French Revolution, which overthrew the monarchy. He was later jailed for opposing the execution of King Louis XVI.

Among Paine's other publications were *The Rights of Man* and *The Age of Reason*. These books helped create a period known as the Enlightenment, during which many people began to explore beyond and question what they had been taught to believe.

Paine was released from prison and returned to America in 1802. He was no longer as popular as he had once been. He began writing articles against the Federalists, the political party that favored a strong central government. He was accused of being an atheist because he opposed organized religion and did not claim to be a Christian.

Newspapers reported Paine's death in New York in 1809 as "a result of the ravages of alcohol and age." He was buried on a farm in New York given to him by the government as payment for his services during the Revolution. Ten years later his remains were taken to England, but officials would not allow him to be buried there. What happened to his remains after that is not known.

ETHAN ALLEN

LEADER OF THE GREEN MOUNTAIN BOYS
1738–1789

There is an original something about Allen that commands attention.

—General George Washington

At six feet, six inches tall, Ethan Allen towered above the ministers and judges in the Salisbury, Connecticut courtroom. It wasn't the first time the bold and proud young man had been arrested. Previous charges against him involved fighting and drinking too much grog (rum punch). The two crimes the rugged frontiersman was accused of committing this day in 1764 were different: Allen had dared to be vaccinated against smallpox virus, and worse still, he had done so on a Sunday. Both were strictly prohibited by laws introduced by the Puritans of New England.

Allen was the oldest of the eight children born to Joseph and Mary Allen near Litchfield, Connecticut. His birth date is believed to be January 21, 1738, although a record in an old family Bible lists his date of birth as January 10, 1737. The family moved to Cornwall, Connecticut. At the time Ethan was growing up, Connecticut was on the frontier between civilization and wilderness. Ethan's physical abilities were legendary: He had tremendous strength, he could endure severe cold, and he could capture deer by outrunning them.

Reading was as important to Allen as was hunting. The more he read, the more he became a believer in the rights of the colonists to establish their own government and that it was wrong for laws to be based on religion. This led to clashes in New England, where church leaders were in charge of the courts.

His father planned for Ethan to attend school at Yale, but Joseph died when Ethan was seventeen, leaving that young man the responsibility of the family farm and caring for his mother and his younger brothers and sisters. Allen married Mary Brownson of Woodbury, Connecticut, in 1762.

In addition to operating the farm, Allen and his brother built the first iron mill and blast furnace in Connecticut. When they sold this business, Allen felt that the buyer did not pay the sum of money they had been promised. Court records state that Allen "with threatening words and angry looks and with force and arms" attacked the buyer. He paid a fine for his actions and gained a reputation as a man with a quick temper who did not hesitate to take action against his enemies.

In the winter of 1767, Allen hiked to the area known as Vermont, from the French words meaning "green mountain." He purchased a thousand acres in an area claimed by both New Hampshire and New York. New York's claim had the

Ethan Allen and the Green Mountain Boys

support of King George III of Britain. Allen quickly became a foe of the "Yorkers," and he gathered volunteers for a militia (citizen soldiers) to defend the independence of the Vermont territory against them. When the governor of New York threatened to drive Allen and his militia all the way back to the mountains, the men adopted the name Green Mountain Boys.

The author Frederick Ungeheur described Allen's militia as "a motley number of the younger men of the hills, hardened hunters and rangers of the mountains." Captains serving under Allen included his cousins, Seth Warner and Remember Baker, along with Robert Cochran, Peleg Sunderland, and Sylvanus Brown. Baker was the oldest and most experienced fighter in the group, which numbered fewer than fifty. Many of the men had served in the French and Indian War (1754–1763) helping the British secure claims in America. All were skilled survivors of the harsh frontier.

Allen became known among the settlers of Vermont as a colonial Robin Hood leading an unruly band of troublemakers. His confidence in his abilities mixed with his hot temper and support for American independence made him a very real threat. When he heard that the king's representative in New York had offered a reward for his capture, Allen responded by offering a reward in a lesser amount for any New York official delivered to Fay's Tavern, a well-known meeting place. "They ain't worth as much as we be," Allen bragged.

When Allen heard that the colonies were officially at war with England, he planned with his Green Mountain Boys to capture Fort Ticonderoga, New York. On May 10, 1775, they arrived in the dark. Catching the British soldiers by surprise, Allen and his men were able to take over the fort without firing a shot. Allen's men also captured the guns and ammunition stored nearby. American general **Henry Knox** would later haul these captured weapons to Boston using ox carts and sleds before the British recaptured the fort.

Allen was captured near Montreal, Canada, and imprisoned for three years in Britain. He made good use of his time there by learning French and reading the writings of men such as **Thomas Paine** and **John Adams**. He wrote several important essays and a book about his life as a captive of the British, which became very popular in 1782.

Allen was freed in a prisoner exchange and returned to America. He immediately went to see General **George Washington**, who made him a colonel in the Continental army. In 1778 Allen tried to get the Continental Congress to recognize Vermont as an independent state. When he did not succeed, he turned to the governor of Canada to have the independent republic of Vermont made a part of that country, which caused some to question his patriotism.

Allen died of a stroke on February 12, 1789, and is buried in Burlington, Vermont. His entire life was focused on being independent. He never became a citizen of the United States, because Vermont did not become the fourteenth state in the union until two years after his death.

MARY KATHERINE GODDARD

FIRST PRINTER OF THE SIGNED DECLARATION OF INDEPENDENCE
1738–1816

If the men who signed the Declaration are traitors as the British say, then I will be a traitor as well.

—Mary Katherine Goddard,
newspaper editorial, 1776

Almost everyone knows **John Hancock**'s name is the first and largest on the **Declaration of Independence**. Few, however, know that a woman's name also appears on the document whose signers pledged "our lives, our fortunes and our sacred honor" to establish a new nation.

A fierce supporter of American independence, Mary Katherine Goddard had used her skills as a newspaper publisher to help persuade the colonists in America to break free from English rule. The Declaration of Independence, with fifty-six signatures, was sent to Goddard's print shop, where she boldly added her name at the bottom as the printer of the copies. She is the only woman to place her name on the first published copy of the Declaration of Independence.

Mary Katherine was born on June 16, 1738, in Connecticut to Giles and Sarah Goddard. Her father was a postmaster. Her mother had more education than most other women in the colonies and encouraged Mary Katherine to study everything that her brother, William, studied. Most girls during this time were not encouraged to learn anything other than skills necessary for taking care of home and family, such as cooking and sewing.

In 1762, after Mr. Goddard's death, Sarah and Mary Katherine moved to Providence, Rhode Island, to work in a printing shop owned by William. They helped him start *The Providence Gazette*. Their mahogany printing press, built by watchmaker Isaac Doolittle, was considered one of the finest in the world.

Goddard published the weekly gazette until 1768, when she moved to Philadelphia to work with William at *The Pennsylvania Chronicle*. She helped her brother publish a series of twelve newspaper articles by John Dickinson, who later became known as the "Penman of the Revolution." The essays, titled "Letters from a Farmer in Pennsylvania to the Inhabitants of the British Colonies," were quickly reprinted in nearly all the other newspapers in America.

While Dickinson did not promote independence at that time, he wrote what Goddard fervently believed: "Let these truths be indelibly impressed on our minds: that we cannot be happy without being free."

Goddard moved to Baltimore in 1773 to take over *The Maryland Journal*, another of William's newspapers. Two years later, while William was busy organizing Baltimore's post office system, the paper's front-page banner proclaimed, "published by M. K. Goddard." *The Journal* earned a reputation as one of the best newspapers in the colonies.

On January 18, 1777, the Continental Congress, established to resist the unfair taxes and laws Britain placed on the American colonies, sent each state a copy of the official Declaration of Independence. In addition to the names of the signers, at the bottom of the copy were five words: "Printed by Mary Katherine Goddard." "If the men who signed the Declaration were traitors as the British say, then I will be a traitor as well," she wrote in a newspaper editorial.

As copies of the Declaration of Independence were circulated throughout the colonies, Goddard continued to edit the *Journal* by herself and was usually Baltimore's only printer. At a time when women could not own property or vote, she believed freedom to do both could come only in a new nation. She kept readers informed as the war progressed, even when her life was threatened by those who were loyal to the British.

A lack of paper presented Goddard more problems during the Revolution that the British did. There were few paper mills in America, and the army needed the paper the mills did produce to make ammunition and for military communication. At times Goddard had to resort to making her own paper, using bits of bleached cloth and scraps of old paper soaked in water, beaten together, and pressed on a screen to dry in flat sheets.

Goddard took over the job of Baltimore postmaster from her brother just before the Revolutionary War began. But in 1789, Postmaster General Samuel Osgood fired her, declaring that the head of the Baltimore postal system must be a man. Goddard had been honest and faithful to her duties for fourteen years, often using her own money to pay the postal riders who carried the mail by horseback. She refused to give up her job without a fight. She secured recommendations from two hundred leading businessmen in Baltimore. She appealed to President **George Washington**, but he would not help her. She petitioned

Congress, but Congress refused to ask the postmaster general to reinstate her. The woman who had been brave enough to put her name on the Declaration of Independence and who influenced thousands for the patriot cause lost the battle to keep her job with the postal service.

Mary Katherine Goddard became a colporteur (seller of religious books) at a bookstore in Baltimore, a job she held until 1802. She died on August 12, 1816. In spite of her bitterness over losing her post office job, she remained devoted to the United States of America, "the nation I helped birth."

NATHANAEL GREENE

FAITHFUL, FIGHTING GENERAL
1742–1786

We fight, get beat, rise, and fight again.

—Nathanael Greene, 1781

General Nathanael Greene had walked with a slight limp all his life. In spite of his limp, in 1775 he became the youngest brigadier general in the Continental army, having earned the respect and trust of his men as well as that of General **George Washington**.

Now, in the bitter cold of Valley Forge, Pennsylvania, in the winter of

1777–1778, Greene faced an even greater challenge. Officers who had once been loyal to Washington were plotting to remove him as commander because they felt he had become a weak leader. They wanted Greene to join them. Greene stepped inside Washington's tent and spoke loudly so that no one misunderstood his loyalty: "General Washington, I am ready to do as you command."

Born on August 7, 1742, Greene was the son of a Quaker minister who owned a blacksmith shop and a mill in Potowomut, Rhode Island. He was schooled at home and learned to read from the Bible. Greene loved reading so much that he began making small toys to sell in order to buy books.

When Greene was a teenager, his father gave him the responsibility of managing the mill. Greene's fairness with customers and quick business sense earned him the respect of his neighbors and led to his election to the General Assembly of Rhode Island. Fighting was against the teachings of his Quaker upbringing. Greene knew, however, that the colonists would have to defend their homes against the British in a war for independence, so he organized a local militia (citizen soldiers) and trained them to use their muskets and rifles in battle.

Washington and Greene met in Boston, and a lifelong friendship began. In December 1776 Greene fought with Washington at the Battle of Trenton in New Jersey, then fought in the battles of Brandywine and Germantown in Pennsylvania.

The situation at Valley Forge in the winter of 1777 was desperate. The army had run out of food, clothing, blankets, medicine, and tents. "No meat! No meat!" the starving soldiers chanted. Cornmeal mush was all the eleven thousand soldiers had to eat.

"You might have tracked the army to Valley Forge by the blood of their feet," General Washington wrote to his brother, adding that he feared the fight for freedom had come to an end. He turned to Greene, who had faithfully stood by him, and gave Greene the assignment to lead the battle against the greatest enemy they had ever faced: starvation.

Greene became the third quartermaster-general of the army. This made him the officer in charge of gathering supplies to feed, clothe, and shelter the men at Valley Forge. Greene approached the challenge with the same determination he had used to prove that his limp would not keep him from leading a fight. Washington later credited him as "the reason for our survival, with the help of Almighty God."

In 1780 Greene resigned as quartermaster-general with Washington's approval. He wanted to concentrate on commanding his troops. Benedict Arnold at this time commanded West Point, an important location on the Hudson River in New York. Arnold betrayed the Americans when he made a secret agreement to turn West Point over to the British major John Andre. When his treason was discovered, Arnold escaped capture, but Andre did not. Greene became the post commander at West Point, which is now the site of the United States Military Academy.

It fell to Greene to take charge of the investigation and trial of Andre. After Andre was found guilty, the British tried to convince Greene to let Andre go. Greene refused. He knew that if he did not carry out the sentence of death given Andre, many more American lives would be lost.

When British troops in South Carolina and Georgia moved to take over North Carolina and Virginia, Washington made Greene commander of the southern army. This put him second in command to Washington. Greene's southern soldiers were ragged, poorly equipped, and discouraged. "I must do something to help these men hold on to their country," Greene told his wife, Catherine. They had married in 1774, and Catherine strongly supported his career as a soldier for the patriot cause.

Greene devised a brilliant plan to stun the British, who assumed that they could easily defeat the southern colonists. On January 17, 1781, he and General Daniel Morgan surrounded the British soldiers led by General Charles Cornwallis at a place in South Carolina known as the Cowpens, where cattle waiting to be sold were penned, similar to today's cattle auction ring.

Most of the British soldiers were captured or killed, and Cornwallis retreated with what was left of his army. Greene and Morgan marched their victorious troops into Virginia in pursuit. In March they met Cornwallis for another battle at Guilford Courthouse in Virginia. Greene lost that battle but managed to severely reduce the number of soldiers in Cornwallis's army.

Just as Greene had not let his limp distract him from preparing the colonists for battle before the war, he did not let this loss detract him from fighting for independence. He returned to South Carolina and within eighteen months captured all of the British posts and took 3,500 prisoners.

When the Revolutionary War ended, Greene retired to a parcel of land near Savannah, Georgia, given him by the grateful people of Georgia and South Carolina. He was the only general besides Washington to have served throughout the entire war. He died of a heat stroke on June 19, 1786, and is buried beneath a monument in Savannah. Buried beside Greene is his oldest son, George Washington Greene, named in honor of the leader and friend Greene had faithfully served.

THOMAS JEFFERSON

ARCHITECT OF FREEDOM
1743–1826

. . . Life, liberty and the pursuit of happiness . . .

—Thomas Jefferson

Thomas Jefferson sat in his study in Washington, D.C. with his feet in a pan of cold water and his pet mockingbird on his shoulder. He was certain his daily habit of soaking his feet in cold water would keep him from catching a bad cold. He reached for the thin vine growing in a nearby basket and gently wrapped it around his finger. For all his accomplishments as an author, architect, inventor, and politician, nothing pleased the third president of the United States more than knowing that he was the first person in America to grow a tomato.

Jefferson was born on April 13, 1743, in Albemarle County, Virginia. The love of agriculture came naturally to the son of farmer Peter Jefferson and his wife, Jane Randolph Jefferson. Their sandy-red-haired, freckle-faced son often played in the fields of Shadwell Plantation. Long before Thomas went to school, he knew how to prepare a survey map. When he was older, he went to live with the Reverend James Maury twelve miles away to attend school. There he learned to keep notes in Greek and Latin in a commonplace book. To write faster, he invented a method of shorthand. At the College of William and Mary in Williamsburg, Virginia, his studies included mathematics, science, French, and the violin. After graduating in 1762, he studied with George Wythe, the greatest teacher of law in colonial America.

In 1768 Jefferson used his skills as an architect to design and begin building a house he called Monticello at the top of an 867-foot mountain. The house was not yet finished when he married Martha Wayles Skelton, a twenty-three-year-old widow. Only two daughters of their six children lived to adulthood.

Jefferson began his political career when he was elected to the Virginia House of Burgesses (representatives). He had been closely involved for several years with the colonists who were protesting British rule, but unlike outspoken leaders for independence such as **Samuel Adams**, **James Otis**, and **Patrick Henry**, Jefferson was not a great public speaker. He preferred to put his thoughts and opinions on paper. In 1774 he wrote *A Summary View of the Rights of British America*, which stressed the natural rights of the colonists not to be ruled by Britain. Word quickly spread among the colonists that Jefferson was a brilliant young patriot and writer. The British considered him a dangerous young rebel.

In 1775 Jefferson was elected to be a delegate from Virginia to the Second Continental Congress. The congress met to unite the colonists against British rule. Jefferson seldom spoke before the congress, but his quill was constantly in motion as he listened and wrote page after page of notes.

In June 1776 **Richard Henry Lee** proposed that a formal declaration of independence be written. Jefferson was named as one of the five men to compose it. Assisted mostly by **John Adams** and **Charles Thomson**, the secretary of the congress, Jefferson completed his draft of the **Declaration of Independence** in just a few days. The members of the Continental Congress made numerous changes to which Jefferson objected, such as his statement against slavery, (though he was a slaveholder), but he signed the final version. He had authored and autographed the birth certificate of the United States of America.

Jefferson returned to Virginia and served in the Virginia legislature until his election as governor in 1779. He became close friends with another member of the Virginia legislature and a future president, **James Madison**. Yet another future president, **James Monroe**, began studying law with Jefferson.

When **Benjamin Franklin** retired as minister to France, Jefferson took his place. He was in France when the **Constitution of the United States of America** was written, debated, and ratified (accepted). He returned to America and became President **George Washington**'s secretary of state. Washington allowed **Alexander Hamilton** to interfere with Jefferson's foreign policy efforts, however, causing Jefferson to resign in 1793.

Jefferson left politics to focus on farming. He felt agriculture was the backbone of the nation. At Monticello he experimented with growing different plants and designed and built a variety of tools, including an iron plow for cutting into hillsides. He returned to politics to run for the presidency in 1796, losing to John Adams. According to the election laws at that time, Jefferson became the vice president. While serving as vice president, he helped design the town of Washington, D.C. He also wrote *A Manual of Parliamentary Procedure*, which established rules for how the Senate was to conduct business in a fair and orderly manner. The Senate followed the rules exactly as Jefferson wrote them until 1993. The manual was then updated; the new version is now used.

Jefferson ran again for the presidency in 1800 and barely won against Aaron Burr to become the third president of the United States. According to the law at the time, state legislators chose the presidential electors. Each elector cast a ballot for both president and vice president without indicating which was for president and which was for vice president. Jefferson and Burr tied, leaving no clear winner. The election was decided in the House of Representatives, which chose Jefferson on the thirty-sixth ballot, to break the tie.

Jefferson was the first president to take the oath of office in the nation's new capital of Washington, D.C. He introduced America to ice cream, waffles, and macaroni and proved that tomatoes were not poisonous, which people in the United States believed. Plans for the Lewis and Clark expedition began during this term, after the Louisiana Purchase by the United States from France in 1803.

Jefferson was elected to a second term as president in 1804. This term was filled with many problems, and Jefferson made several unpopular decisions. He left public office when his term ended and devoted the rest of his life to his family, reading, writing, and education. In 1814 he sold his collection of 6,487 books to the Library of Congress. Another thousand volumes were given to the University of Virginia when he died. One of his greatest joys had been designing the University of Virginia, and in 1976 the American Institute of Architects voted his design "the proudest achievement of American architecture in the past two hundred years."

Jefferson wrote more than eighteen thousand letters and documents and accumulated more than twenty-five thousand letters and documents from friends. A number of these letters were written after he and John Adams resumed their friendship, which had been disrupted following the election of 1800. In their letters they often referred to the extraordinary experiences they shared during their days together in the Continental Congress, when they wrote the Declaration of Independence.

Celebrations were held across the nation on July 4, 1826, to mark the fiftieth anniversary of the signing of the Declaration of Independence. Neither Thomas Jefferson nor John Adams was able to attend them. Jefferson died peacefully just after noon that day at Monticello. Adams died a few hours later at his farm in Massachusetts.

JOHN JAY

FIRST JUSTICE OF THE SUPREME COURT
1745–1829

he people who own the country ought to govern it.

—John Jay

John Jay was one of many people living in the American colonies who believed in individual freedoms but did not want independence from Britain. Once the Revolutionary War was under way, however, Jay stepped forward to boldly support the patriot cause.

Jay was born in New York City on December 12, 1745, to Peter and Mary

Van Cortlandt Jay. Peter, a successful merchant, wanted to give his children the best life had to offer. He sent John to an exclusive boarding school when he was eight, and when John was fourteen, he went to King's College, which is now Columbia University. He graduated with highest honors and went to a law office to study law. By 1768 he had a thriving law practice of his own.

"Obtaining a proper legal education in the colonies was made most difficult due to the lack of necessary books. Those who study in England have more than 150 volumes of English law reports. In the colonies we have fewer than thirty," Jay explained when he could not provide answers for some of the colonists' problems.

Jay become active in politics and went to the first meeting of the Continental Congress to represent New York. The Continental Congress was established to unite the colonists to resist British taxes and laws that they felt were unfair. At twenty-eight Jay was the second-youngest member.

Jay sided with delegates who wanted to settle problems with Britain peacefully. Other delegates wanted to go to war immediately. They agreed in July 1775 to have Jay write a letter they called "the Olive Branch Petition" to King George asking Britain to change the laws that made life difficult for the colonists. King George refused even to consider the petition.

Jay did not want to give up hope for a peaceful solution. When the Continental Congress declared independence from Britain, Jay was deliberately absent and did not sign the **Declaration of Independence**. He resigned from Congress and returned to New York, where he became chief justice of the state supreme court.

By 1778 Jay had given up hope of peace with Britain and joined in supporting the war. He was reelected to the Continental Congress. The other delegates elected him president of the congress the day he arrived.

Congress knew a young nation declaring independence needed outside support. In 1779 Jay went to Spain to persuade the Spanish government to endorse the fight for independence and to give America money to finance the revolution. Louisiana Spanish governor **Bernardo de Gálvez** contributed greatly to the financial needs of the patriots.

After the British surrendered, Jay went to Paris with **Benjamin Franklin** and **John Adams** to meet with a British representative and negotiate a peace treaty. The four men worked out an agreement favorable to the United States, and Jay returned to America. When he got home, he learned that Congress had named him secretary of state for foreign affairs.

Jay teamed up with **James Madison** and **Alexander Hamilton** in 1787 to write *The Federalist Papers* in support of the new **Constitution of the United States of America**. Jay did not know that the articles he co-wrote, which appeared under the pen name **Publius**, would become famous all over the world for explaining and defending the U.S. Constitution.

The Constitution created three branches of government—executive, legislative, and judicial. Article III of the Constitution created the Supreme Court of the United States. The Supreme Court would be the final court a person could bring a case before, after other courts had heard the case.

Congress decided that the Supreme Court should have a chief justice and five associate justices and that the court would meet in New York City, then the nation's capital. The president of the United States had the power to appoint the justices with the advice and consent of the Senate. President **George Washington** immediately appointed John Jay the first chief justice of the Supreme Court.

The Judiciary Act of 1789 required the judges to travel around the country twice a year to hear cases. Congress thought the justices needed to stay in touch with local opinion and state laws. This system might have worked with today's transportation systems. For Jay and the other judges, however, the travel was something between difficult and intolerable. The longest trips took about nineteen hours in a stagecoach. Some roads were little more than trails. It took 101 years for Congress to end this system and allow the Supreme Court to meet in one place all year.

When Britain did not abide by the terms of the peace treaty with the United States of America, President Washington asked Jay to step down from the Supreme Court and go to England to resolve the continuing problems between the two countries. After returning to America, Jay served as governor of New York. He worked hard for the abolition (elimination) of slavery and to improve New York's economy, roads, and canals.

Jay retired from public life in 1801. Both he and his wife, Sarah Livingston Jay, were in poor health. President John Adams tried to reappoint him to the Supreme Court, but Jay refused. Though the last few years of his life were physically uncomfortable, his mind remained sharp.

"I am happy to be surrounded by friends and family and so many books," he said shortly before his death on May 17, 1829. He is buried in the John Jay Cemetery in Rye, New York.

BENJAMIN RUSH

SURGEON GENERAL OF THE
CONTINENTAL ARMY
1745–1813

The Revolutionary War may be over, but the battle of independence has just begun.

—Dr. Benjamin Rush, 1782

Benjamin Rush eagerly placed his signature on the document declaring independence for the American colonies, but he knew signing his name was not enough. The thirty-year-old doctor, who only a few months earlier had married seventeen-year-old Julia Stockton, told his new bride, "There is but one other thing for me to do to show my support for independence. To save the lives of soldiers, I must become a soldier myself."

Benjamin Rush was born to John and Susanna Harvey Rush on December 24, 1745. He and his seven brothers and sisters lived with their parents on a plantation near Byberry, Pennsylvania. When Benjamin was six, his father died. For a while his mother supported the family as a costermonger (a person who sold fruits and vegetables). She soon sent Benjamin to live with his uncle, Dr. Samuel Finley, who enrolled Benjamin in his school in Maryland. Benjamin learned so quickly that he went straight from his uncle's academy to the junior class at the University of New Jersey (now Princeton University) when he was only thirteen.

After graduating from Princeton, Rush studied medicine with a local doctor. Doctors in colonial days were known as "leeches" because the most common method of treating a sick person at that time was to "bleed" a patient. Actual parasitic leeches were used to draw blood. This was supposed to get rid of disease, but of course it did not.

In 1766 Rush went to Edinburgh, Scotland, to study medicine. He earned his medical degree two years later. After he returned to Philadelphia, his strong political opinions and friendships with some of the leading revolutionaries helped him become elected as a Pennsylvania delegate (representative) to the Second Continental Congress. The Continental Congress had been established to resist the unfair taxes and laws Britain placed on the American colonies. Rush voted for independence and signed the **Declaration of Independence**, the only physician to do so.

Rush voluntarily joined the Continental army and became surgeon general (highest-ranking doctor) in April 1777. Medical treatment on the battlefields was terrible. There were few supplies, and surgeries were done under very unsanitary conditions with no anesthetics.

Rush became increasingly unhappy about the poor sanitary conditions in the army camps and had many arguments with General **George Washington**. Rush wrote a letter to his friend **Patrick Henry**, criticizing Washington as a poor leader. Later, he admitted he was wrong in his harsh complaints about Washington, and they became good friends.

In 1778 Rush returned to practicing medicine in Philadelphia. He joined the staff at Pennsylvania Hospital, where men who were suffering mentally as well as physically from the horrors of war were often treated as criminals. Rush knew these men and others with mental illnesses needed kindness and compassion. He studied mental illness for the thirty years he worked at the hospital and wrote the first textbook on psychiatry (the study of the mind) in America.

Rush briefly re-entered politics in 1787 to urge Pennsylvania to ratify (agree to) the **Constitution of the United States of America**. He believed it offered the best hope for creating a government strong enough to care both mentally and physically for the victims of the war.

In 1793 a yellow fever epidemic broke out in Philadelphia. Yellow fever, also known as Barbados fever or black vomit, is transmitted by mosquitoes, which are attracted to areas with stagnant water. Rush urged Pennsylvania authorities to adopt better sanitation methods to stop the disease. By 1805 his studies with improving sanitation to stop the spread of disease were widely read not only in the United States, but also in Europe. The king of Prussia even awarded Rush a medal for teaching the people of Europe how to stop yellow fever from spreading.

Although his father had been a slave owner, Rush opposed keeping slaves. He wrote a pamphlet attacking the slave trade and those who owned slaves. Rush wrote the constitution for the Pennsylvania Abolition (end of all slavery) Society, which worked to end slavery, and served as the group's president.

Slavery was not the only issue that Rush used his superb writing skills to address. He believed that women deserved the same education as men and that all children should receive free public education. The Bible, Rush urged, should be used as a teaching tool in every school, and he founded the Bible Society in

America. "A republican nation can never be long free and happy unless its citizens are educated," he wrote.

In 1797 President **John Adams** appointed Rush as treasurer of the U.S. Mint. Adams wanted only the most trustworthy person to be in control of making and distributing the nation's money. Rush held that position until he died of typhoid fever—a disease spread by contaminated water—in 1813. He is buried at Christ Church in Philadelphia.

In 1965 the American Psychiatric Association put a bronze plaque on Dr. Rush's grave, identifying him as the "Father of American Psychiatry." Of all his patriotic accomplishments, it is the recognition he most likely would have been the proudest to have received.

ANTHONY WAYNE

FOUND WHEREVER THERE WAS A FIGHT
1745–1796

The Americans are now led by a chief who never sleeps. In spite of the watchfulness of our braves, we have never been able to surprise him.

—Little Turtle of the Miami Indians describing General Anthony Wayne

No matter how difficult or dangerous the assignment, Anthony Wayne devoted himself to getting the job done. He earned the loyalty of the men he led by never asking them to do what he would not do himself. Historians say he was given the nickname "Mad Anthony" when a soldier at Valley Forge, Pennsylvania, became so unruly that Wayne sentenced him to receive twenty-nine lashes. The soldier responded by shouting over and over, "Anthony is mad, stark mad." The name stuck.

Wayne was born on January 1, 1745, in Chester County, Pennsylvania. He was the only son of Isaac and Elizabeth Iddings Wayne. His favorite boyhood pastime was to reenact battles. His teacher told his father that Anthony did not have the talent to be a scholar, "but perhaps a soldier."

Anthony did well enough in math to attend the Philadelphia Academy and become a land surveyor (someone who sets land boundaries). **Benjamin Franklin** hired him for his first surveying job, where he learned skills that would later help him construct four important forts in the western territories.

Wayne became a representative to the Pennsylvania colonial legislature in 1774. He was also a member that year of the First Continental Congress, which met to consider what to do about the worsening relationship between the colonies and Britain.

When the Revolutionary War broke out, Wayne organized the Fourth Regiment of Pennsylvania and was commissioned (given the authority of) a colonel on January 3, 1776. Just over a year later he was promoted to brigadier general and assigned to serve under General **George Washington**.

At the Battle of Brandywine in Pennsylvania in September 1777, Wayne successfully defended an area called Chadd's Ford against the Hessians. The Hessians were German soldiers hired by the British to fight for them. A few days later Wayne encountered the enemy just outside Philadelphia. This time he was badly outnumbered. British soldiers killed 158 of his men with bayonets. When accusers blamed Wayne for the disaster, Wayne asked for a military court of inquiry. The court found him innocent of neglecting his duty and returned him to his position "with the highest honor."

Wayne spent the winter of 1777–1778 at Valley Forge, Pennsylvania. The camp at Valley Forge did not have adequate supplies, so Wayne led carefully planned raids on British camps and came away with horses, cattle, and other goods the patriot army desperately needed. "Without Wayne's cunning bravery, we would all have been dead men," General Washington said.

At the Battle of Monmouth in New Jersey in June 1778, Wayne was the first to attack. General Charles Lee ordered him back, but when General Washington arrived, Wayne was allowed to resume his attack and was victorious.

During the summer of 1779, General Washington asked Wayne to command a corps of light infantry (foot soldiers). Wayne and his men then captured Stony Point, New York, a post on the Hudson River that was an important river crossing for north-south traffic. Wayne had decided to storm the fort in a midnight raid. The surprise attack ended with few of his soldiers killed and a quick surrender by the British.

"Our officers and men behaved like men who were determined to be free," Wayne wrote to Washington. Wayne was wounded in the battle and received a medal for his extraordinary success.

Wherever there was fighting or trouble, Anthony Wayne could be found. He was sent to Georgia to drive the British out, then to South Carolina where he served under General **Nathanael Greene** in 1781. His service did not end when the Revolutionary War ended. Britain had agreed that the western boundary of the United States would be the Mississippi River stretching north to the Great Lakes. However, the British failed to withdraw their troops from the western region. Instead, they provided weapons to the Indians in exchange for furs.

Native Americans had inhabited the Ohio Valley for many generations and had formed an alliance to meet the threat of the settlers pushing into their lands. They were encouraged by the British to increase their attacks on settlers.

In the summer of 1794, Wayne and his troops were sent into the Ohio Valley, where they raided and destroyed Indian villages. Little Turtle, the leader of the Indian alliance, wanted to negotiate with Wayne for peace but was replaced by Blue Jacket, who decided to stand and fight, not negotiate, with the man the Indians called "Blacksnake" because of his sudden strike tactics.

On August 20, 1794, Wayne attacked the Indians at Fallen Timbers, just south of Toledo, Ohio, and forced them to retreat toward British protection. The British, not wanting another war with the United States, declined to protect them. Wayne's victory at Fallen Timbers marked the end of the problems with the British in the West and was considered his greatest military success. Shortly after, President Washington appointed General Wayne to be commander in chief of the U.S. Army. Wayne died from kidney disease on December 16, 1796. He was buried near Erie, Pennsylvania.

Even death could not end the story of the dedicated patriot, however. Thirteen years after Wayne's death, his son, Isaac, decided to move the body to the family plot more than three hundred miles away in Radnor, Pennsylvania. The people of Erie did not want to lose the body of the brilliant war hero, so Dr. James Wallace separated Wayne's flesh from his bones. The flesh was reburied near Erie, and the skeleton was taken to Radnor. According to legends, some of the bones fell out of the wagon carrying them to Radnor, and the ghost of Mad Anthony Wayne is still searching for them along the road.

BERNARDO DE GÁLVEZ

HISPANIC HERO OF THE REVOLUTION
1746–1786

May this statue of Bernardo de Gálvez serve as a reminder that Spain offered the blood of her soldiers for the cause of American independence.

—Inscription on monument honoring
Bernardo de Gálvez in Washington, D.C.

For three years Louisiana governor Bernardo de Gálvez secretly helped the Americans in their fight for independence by keeping the Mississippi

River flowing with men, ammunition, and supplies desperately needed in the north and east by the patriots. When Spain officially declared war against the British in 1779, Gálvez rose to the challenge of raising his own army to fight the British.

His letter to Spanish Texas governor Domingo Cabello y Robles, however, did not ask for men or weapons. "Gálvez asked for ten thousand head of cattle to feed his soldiers," Robles told Texas ranchers and vaqueros (Spanish cowboys). "And ten thousand head of cattle he shall have!"

Bernardo de Gálvez was born near Malaga, Spain, on July 23, 1746. His parents, Matias and Josepha Madrid y Gallardo de Gálvez, were part of a family well known for its service to Spain. By age sixteen Bernardo was serving in the Spanish army in a war with Portugal. In 1769 he was sent to New Spain (America) to fight against the Apache Indians.

Gálvez returned to Spain to improve his military education. He was sent back to America in 1776 and assigned to the Louisiana Province, which at that time was owned by Spain. A year later he became the governor of Louisiana, where he met and married Marie Felice de Saint-Maxent Estrehan. His mission as governor was to fight smuggling and promote commerce by bringing settlers from Spain and many other countries to the province. He gave land, cattle, and farm implements to each family, provided money and supplies, and ordered a church to be built for each settlement. Gálvez encouraged the people of Louisiana to trade with the American colonists.

Throughout the first three years of the American Revolution, **Thomas Jefferson** and **Patrick Henry** trusted the shrewd and courageous Gálvez to keep the British out of the port of New Orleans. They knew that if the Mississippi River came under British control, the Americans would lose the war.

Gálvez did more than keep the British out of the port of New Orleans. Fueled by the beef provided by the ranchers and vaqueros from Texas, he and his army defeated the British at Baton Rouge, Louisiana; at Natchez in what is now Mississippi; and at the British naval base at Mobile Bay. In the spring of 1780,

Gálvez boldly advanced up the Mississippi toward the Great Lakes, defeating every British-held post along the river. This cleared the way for supplies to continue reaching General **George Rogers Clark** and General **George Washington**, who were fighting the British in the north and the east.

In 1781 Gálvez led seven thousand men to Pensacola, which was the British capital of Florida. Fort Half Moon, seven miles from Pensacola, was heavily armed and protected by the British with giant cannons pointed seaward. Everyone thought Fort Half Moon could not be taken. Everyone except for Bernardo de Gálvez, that is. With an army made up of Native Americans and soldiers from Spain, Cuba, Mexico, Puerto Rico, and France, and with forty ships he had equipped with guns for close-range attack, he shut off the British from the sea. Then Gálvez boldly sailed his flagship *under* the British guns "right into their front door," as one of the sailors later said. At the end of the battle, 1,100 British troops surrendered, and British military activity was ended in the Gulf of Mexico.

When Gálvez and his ships arrived in Virginia, he knew immediately it would take more than military strategy to finish the defeat of the British. General Washington had cornered General Charles Cornwallis at Yorktown, New York; however, the American army had not been paid in six months except with the paper money printed by the Continental Congress. This money was worthless, and many soldiers were refusing to fight. "I know where to get the gold you must have to pay the men," Gálvez assured Washington.

Gálvez took four ships to Havana, Cuba, where he persuaded the people to help fund the Americans. He collected gold wedding rings, bowls, and even gold and silver crosses from churches and brought them back to Washington to pay the troops. The goods were worth $6 million at the time; that amount would be $120 million in today's money. Gálvez then turned over his never-defeated soldiers to fight with Washington's army at Yorktown.

Gálvez helped draft the terms of the peace treaty that ended the

Revolutionary War. Then he, his wife, and their two children returned to Spain. In 1784 he was sent to Cuba as its governor, and the next year the king of Spain appointed him viceroy (head) of Mexico. Gálvez ordered a mapmaker to make a detailed survey map of the Gulf Coast. The mapmaker named the biggest bay on the Texas coast Bahía de Galvezton. The spelling was later changed to Galveston.

Gálvez completed building the Metropolitan Cathedral in Mexico City, the largest cathedral in the western hemisphere. When he died of an illness in 1786, his body was placed next to his father's in a crypt in San Bernadino, but his heart was placed in an urn kept at the cathedral. In 1980 the U.S. Postal Service issued a stamp in his honor, and his birthday is celebrated as Gálvez Day in several cities. He is remembered not only as a brilliant soldier, but also as a great leader who united people of many cultures to help win America's independence.

TADEUSZ KOSCIUSZKO

POLISH ENGINEER FOR FREEDOM
1746–1817

He is as pure a son of liberty as I have ever known.

—**Thomas Jefferson**,
speaking of Tadeusz Kosciuszko

The jubilant sounds of cheering soldiers filled Tadeusz Kosciuszko's ears. "Their ships are now our targets!"

Kosciuszko, the engineer from Poland who had come to America to help the colonies win independence from Britain, had not fired a shot. Yet the soldiers at Fort Mercer were praising him for the American victory in 1776 over the British navy in the port of Philadelphia.

Born February 12, 1746, in Brest, then in Poland (now in Belarus), Kosciuszko preferred playing with dirt and sticks to playing with toy swords when he was a boy. He studied military engineering in Poland, as well as in Germany, Italy, and France. In 1766 he graduated from the Polish Military Academy and became an instructor at the school.

Kosciuszko sailed for America in 1776, just as the Americans were issuing the **Declaration of Independence**. He applied to the Continental Congress for a commission as an officer, telling General **George Washington**, "I have come to fight as a volunteer for America's independence."

The victory in Philadelphia was the first display of Kosciuszko's genius for designing and building defenses to slow or stop a mighty naval fleet. It confirmed the trust of many Americans who had not been entirely sure of his devotion to their cause. Kosciuszko had proven "engineering warfare" to be as important as any other weapon the Americans were to use in the War of Independence.

After the success at Philadelphia, Washington sent Kosciuszko to improve the defenses of Fort Ticonderoga, located in New York, where Lake Champlain and the Hudson River meet. Ticonderoga was positioned to interrupt the British army traveling the waterways between New York and Canada. Unfortunately, the fort's commander ignored Kosciuszko's recommendation to protect an adjoining hill with a cannon or other artillery. As a result the British captured the fort. This loss convinced the American leaders to trust Kosciuszko's knowledge and tactics.

Kosciuszko played an important role in the battles of Saratoga, New York, in the fall of 1777. The two battles marked a turning point in the war in favor of the Americans. Kosciuszko was asked to choose a position to fortify, or strengthen, with American defenses. He chose Bemis Heights on the Hudson River south of Saratoga. On September 19 the British attacked Saratoga, and the Americans had to retreat to Bemis Heights. That was the first Battle of Saratoga. On October 7 the British attacked again, this time at Bemis Heights. After suffering heavy losses, the British retreated and were surrounded by American troops, who forced the British to surrender on October 17. The American victory at Saratoga was another example of Kosciuszko's shrewd engineering skills, and it encouraged the French to aid the Americans.

The Americans next chose to fortify a place further south on the Hudson River known as West Point. There was no doubt now in General Washington's mind as to who would be in charge of engineering the defenses there.

The "point" in "West Point" is a sharp bend in the Hudson River that force ships to perform a perilous turn when sailing up the river. Part of Kosciuszko's plan for fortification was to submerge a chain across the river. As a ship approached, the chain could be raised to snag it, making the ship a sitting target for the Americans. It was a perfect plan until Benedict Arnold passed the information on to the British. This earned Arnold, who had previously fought for the Americans, the label of "traitor."

While at West Point, Kosciuszko was given a slave named Agrippa Hull. The Polish engineer, who believed in every man's right to liberty, promptly freed Hull, but Hull chose to stay with him to serve.

In August 1780 Kosciuszko was named chief engineer of the Army of the South. In addition to being in charge of engineering, he commanded troops in the field and was wounded in hand-to-hand combat.

After the Revolutionary War ended, Kosciuszko returned to Poland, where he fought against Russian invaders. He was captured and imprisoned for two years. After regaining his freedom, he returned to America, now the United States of America.

Congress gave Kosciuszko a grant of land in Ohio as well as a pension (a regular payment of money in recognition of past services). He died on October 15, 1817, after a fall from a horse. In his will he ordered that the land in Ohio granted to him by Congress be sold, and the proceeds used for the education of African Americans. Even after his death, he wanted to continue helping others in their struggles to be free.

JOHN PAUL JONES

FATHER OF THE AMERICAN NAVY
1747–1792

T hoisted with my own hands the flag of freedom.

—John Paul Jones

Was he a patriot or a pirate? John Paul Jones may have been a little of both. Regardless, his friends and his foes agreed that he was one of the best seamen alive and that he used his skill and talent to help America win the War of Independence.

John was born on July 6, 1747, to John and Jean Paul in Kirkcudbright, Scotland. He and his older brother and three older sisters lived near a large estate where his father was a gardener. He studied math, reading, writing, Latin, and French in school, and at age thirteen he signed on as an apprentice (trainee) seaman aboard the *Friendship*, a merchant ship.

All ships during this time were powered by wind. Ropes tied to the sails controlled the direction in which the ship would sail. The sailors had to know which ropes controlled which sail. John Paul learned fast, and by the time he was sixteen, he was hired to command another merchant ship.

Sailors found John Paul a hard man to work for. He was accused on several occasions of killing crew members. When he was in the West Indies, his crew tried to take over his ship. He killed the leader of the mutiny, later writing in a letter to **Benjamin Franklin** that this was "the greatest misfortune of my life." He claimed that he rowed ashore to turn himself in to authorities, and that his friends advised him to flee to America while he was waiting for a court hearing.

John Paul arrived in America in 1774 and added "Jones" to his name. He intended to become a farmer. Instead, the "little Jones," as **Thomas Jefferson** described him, referring to his height of barely five feet, five inches, decided to join America's new Continental navy. Some believe he saw the coming Revolutionary War as an opportunity to become a hero. Others say he knew his sailing skills were desperately needed to help the struggling Americans win independence.

Jones soon achieved several important firsts. On December 3, 1775, he hoisted the Grand Union Flag of America on his ship. He was the first to raise an American flag on an American warship. On December 7, 1775, he was commissioned the first lieutenant in the Continental navy. On August 8, 1776, he received the first captain's commission after the signing of the **Declaration of Independence**. The declaration stated the colonies were no longer under British rule.

Wherever he went, Jones dressed well and carried a sword. He was very popular socially, though he never married. He was the first seaman to write a list of qualities and characteristics of the ideal naval officer, which included the ability to write well.

On June 14, 1777, Jones earned command of the ship *Ranger* the same day that Congress approved the design for the original Stars and Stripes. Five months later the *Ranger* set out to sea with Captain John Paul Jones in command. When he arrived in France, he gave a thirteen-gun salute to a French ship. When the French ship returned the salute, John recorded it in his captain's log. That was the first recorded admission by a foreign navy that the United States was an independent country.

In 1779 Jones was placed in command of a fleet of American and French ships. He renamed one of the French ships *Bonhomme Richard* ("Good Man Richard") in honor of Benjamin Franklin. When he encountered British merchant ships off the British coast, Jones tied the *Bonhomme Richard* to a much larger British ship, the *Serapis*. For the next three hours the British tried to get him to surrender as the two ships fired into each other.

"I have not yet begun to fight," Jones replied.

More than three hours later, the *Serapis* surrendered, and Jones was hailed a hero in both Paris and Philadelphia. By age thirty-two he had the most distinguished war record of all the American navy's captains. His great popularity, however, made him a target of political jealousy.

Jones served in the Continental navy without getting paid. He called himself a defender of liberty, but he often took enemy merchant ships as prizes. He argued with Congress for his share of the money he felt he was owed for capturing these ships, and eventually he left the American navy. He then served a short time as an admiral in the Russian navy.

John Paul Jones died in Paris on July 18, 1792. More than a hundred years later in 1899, the American president Theodore Roosevelt convinced Congress to fund a search to recover Jones's body from France. Six years later Jones's grave was found in an old cemetery over which buildings had been constructed. Jones's coffin was draped with an American flag and taken through the Paris streets for an official farewell. He was reburied on January 26, 1913, in a tomb under the U.S. Naval Academy chapel in Annapolis, Maryland.

CASIMIR PULASKI

FATHER OF THE AMERICAN CAVALRY
1747–1779

I came here, where freedom is being defended, to serve it, and to live or die for it.

—Casimir Pulaski

A statue of Casimir Pulaski stands in one of the garden squares of Savannah, Georgia. A 1931 two-cent stamp bears his portrait, and a 1979 commemorative postcard depicts him galloping on his horse. His name appears on streets, bridges, schools, and museums across the United States, though few Americans know why.

Casimir Pulaski was born in Poland on March 4, 1747. His father, Josef, was deeply involved in Polish politics. By the time Casimir was fifteen, he had learned several languages. He began training with other Polish noblemen to be a soldier to help stop Russia's efforts to control Poland. By the time he was twenty-one, he commanded a unit of soldiers, an experience that proved extremely important when he later joined the American Revolution.

In October 1771 Pulaski became involved in a plot to capture Poland's Russian king. The plot failed, but he was sentenced to death for his participation. Fortunately, he had already left the country. He went to Turkey to help in another unsuccessful fight against Russia and then fled to France, where he met **Benjamin Franklin** in 1777. America had declared independence from Britain the previous year, and Franklin asked Pulaski to join with the colonists in the revolution. Franklin knew the American army was desperate for leaders like Pulaski, who knew how to unite different groups of people to fight against a common enemy.

Pulaski agreed. Perhaps he wanted another opportunity to prove he was a good leader. It was certain that if he returned to Poland, he would face a death sentence. His reputation across Europe as a person who believed in freedom and independence convinced Franklin to give him a letter of recommendation to take to General **George Washington**, the commander in chief of the Continental army.

Pulaski arrived at Washington's headquarters in Philadelphia late in the summer of 1777. General Washington's army lacked both supplies and money to pay soldiers. Like fellow Polish soldier **Tadeusz Kosciuszko**, who had arrived a year earlier to help the American War of Independence, Pulaski volunteered to serve without pay. Washington welcomed the well-mannered soldier, but other American military leaders did not. They were jealous of the strong nobleman from Poland who had so much more experience than they had.

Pulaski soon proved his worth. He rallied the Americans by leading a counter-attack at the Battle of Brandywine in Pennsylvania, keeping the American defeat from becoming a complete disaster. After this stunning display of courage, Washington wrote a letter to Congress requesting that Pulaski be made a brigadier general and the commander of the cavalry (horse-mounted) troops. "This gentleman has been, like us, engaged in defending the liberty and independence of his country and has sacrificed his fortune," Washington wrote.

The Continental Congress appointed Pulaski general of the cavalry on September 15, 1777. The other Continental army officers did not understand that Pulaski wanted the cavalry to be a separate combat unit from the infantry (foot soldiers), and they were infuriated because a soldier from a foreign country had been given such a high command.

Like Kosciuszko, **Marquis de Lafayette**, and **Baron Friedrich von Steuben**, Pulaski battled poverty as well as prejudice while serving in the Continental army. His men faced constant shortages of food, clothing, and weapons. Lack of clean drinking water and medical care killed almost as many American soldiers as the British army did.

In 1778 a discouraged Pulaski asked Washington to be relieved of his command. He told Washington he would retire rather than continue to struggle with the shortages, even though he'd been successful in several campaigns. Washington persuaded him to stay by convincing Congress to let Pulaski recruit a "corps of lancers" for an independent cavalry unit. Pulaski recruited Americans, Frenchmen, Poles, and even deserters from the Hessian (German) troops fighting for the British. He trained them to fight on horseback with swords as well as with guns. Thirteen Polish officers led these soldiers on horseback in a unit that became known as Pulaski's Legion. A British officer later called them "the best cavalry the rebels ever had."

In February of 1779, Pulaski's Legion numbered about six hundred men. They were sent to South Carolina to stop the steadily advancing British, who already occupied Georgia. The British greatly outnumbered Pulaski and his cavalry, but the Polish volunteer won a surprise victory that stopped the British and boosted the spirits of the Americans.

Pulaski was determined to recapture the territory held by the British. On October 9 his troops, along with French troops, attacked British-occupied Savannah, where they were met by heavy British fire. Pulaski's soldiers began to scatter. As he rushed forward on his horse, trying to regroup them, he was hit by cannon fire. His men carried him to the warship *Wasp* in Savannah Harbor. Pulaski died there two days later, on October 11, 1779. He was only thirty-two years old. The gallant Polish commander who established the American cavalry was buried at sea.

HENRY KNOX

THE "OX" OF THE REVOLUTIONARY WAR
1750–1806

He is too valuable to me.

—General George Washington,
describing Henry Knox

Henry Knox looked up from the manual of military strategy he was reading in his Boston bookstore in 1774. The young woman who had just entered was the daughter of a devoted British Loyalist, and Knox knew her father did not want her in his store. She had, in fact, been told that she must choose between her family and her love for Knox, who was a poor shopkeeper and a member of Massachusetts's rebel militia (citizen soldiers.) Unknown to her father, the choice had already been made. Henry Knox and Lucy Fluker had secretly wed, and they were ready to join other young patriots in the battle for America's independence.

Henry Knox was born on July 25, 1750, the seventh of ten children born to William and Mary Campbell Knox. His father was a shipmaster who died when Henry was nine. With limited education and no money, Henry went to work as a clerk in a bookstore when he was about twelve years old to help support his family. His love of reading led him to open a bookstore of his own when he was twenty.

After the battles of Lexington and Concord in Massachusetts in the spring of 1775, Knox left his bookstore and joined other volunteers fighting the British at the Battle of Bunker Hill, also in Massachusetts. The loss of two fingers on his left hand in a hunting accident several years earlier did not slow him down in this first large-scale battle of the American Revolution. His gallant service earned him the rank of colonel from General **George Washington**, who was impressed with the tremendous knowledge of artillery (heavy guns and cannons) that Knox had gained through reading. He presented a daring plan to Washington: Bring the cannons that **Ethan Allen** had helped capture at Fort Ticonderoga, New York, near the Canadian border, to Boston. Everyone warned Washington that Knox's plan to move fifty-nine cannons weighing sixty tons almost three hundred miles through rough territory was impossible. Desperate for artillery, Washington agreed to Knox's plan.

Knox set out in November 1775, when heavy snow covered the ground. With two thousand men, forty-two sleds loaded with the cannons, and four hundred oxen pulling them, he arrived on March 4, 1776, at Dorchester Heights in Boston. Two weeks later the British abandoned the city, and twenty-five-year-old Knox became a national hero.

General George Washington and troops cross the Delaware River following the callouts by Henry Knox

Washington often turned to Knox to help find money to pay the soldiers when the Continental Congress had none. On one occasion Knox obtained fifty thousand dollars from the businessman **Robert Morris**. On other occasions he persuaded the citizens of the New England colonies to provide supplies to keep the Continental army fighting. "Knox could solve problems as quickly as he consumed bread," fellow officers teased, referring to Knox's weight of more than 250 pounds.

On Christmas night of 1776, Knox stood in the darkness on the shore of the Delaware River and, using only his voice, directed Washington and the troops struggling in small boats through the floating ice of the river to safety. Knox then led the charge through a blinding snowstorm against the camp of the Hessian (German) soldiers at the Battle of Trenton, in New Jersey, after which he was promoted to brigadier general.

During the bitter winter at Valley Forge, Pennsylvania, Knox worked with **Baron Friedrich von Steuben** drilling troops and with **Nathanael Greene** obtaining more supplies and building forts to protect the ragtag, ill-equipped American army. His assignments as chief of artillery of the Continental army read like a time line of the Revolutionary War: He fought in the battles of Princeton, Brandywine, and Germantown in 1777; he fought at the Battle of Monmouth in 1778; and he set the artillery in place for the Battle of Yorktown in 1781.

Lucy accompanied her husband to many of his assignments—the family, which eventually included thirteen children, moved fourteen times in nineteen years. Her calm and generous personality made "Madame Knox" a welcome presence wherever Knox was assigned.

When the Revolutionary War ended, Major General Knox commanded the West Point fortress in New York and was elected secretary of war by Congress. When the **Constitution of the United States of America** was ratified (accepted) in 1787, Knox wrote a letter to Washington urging him to accept the job as president. Knox told Washington that he would be remembered as "the father of our country" if he became the first president. Washington, who referred to his old friend as "Ox Knox," finally agreed.

Knox wanted to retire from public service, but President Washington asked him to serve as his secretary of war for the new United States of America. Knox had never refused a request from Washington. He again offered his skills as a problem-solver to help negotiate treaties with the Indians.

Knox retired to his farm in Thomaston, Maine, in 1796. He built Lucy the home he had promised her for all she had endured "as an artillery officer's wife." While enjoying a meal with friends at their home, he swallowed a chicken bone that probably punctured his intestine. He died two days later, on October 25, 1806, and is buried beside Lucy in Thomaston.

THE LIBERTY BELL

A CHIME THAT CHANGED THE WORLD
1751–PRESENT

Proclaim liberty throughout the land unto all the inhabitants thereof.

—Inscription engraved on the Liberty Bell from Leviticus 25:10, King James Bible

The wagon groaned beneath the weight of its load. The horses strained forward in their harnesses. "Be on your way," a muffled voice instructed the wagon driver. Surrounded by the darkness of a September night in 1777, the Liberty Bell, then known as the Great Bell, lay hidden beneath the hay in the wagon. The driver knew that if he were captured carrying the bell from Philadelphia to Northampton (now Allentown), Pennsylvania, the 2,080-pound bell would be melted into shot (bullets) for the British, and he would become another American casualty of the Revolutionary War.

The first Liberty Bell was ordered in 1751 as part of the celebration planned for the fiftieth anniversary of William Penn's Charter of Privileges. Penn's charter, which listed people's rights and freedoms, served as the first constitution (system of rules and laws) of Pennsylvania. The Pennsylvania Assembly wanted a bell to hang in the new tower of the State House in Philadelphia (now Independence Hall) to ring in celebration of the liberty they enjoyed.

Assembly Leader Isaac Norris described the State House as "a building coming out of the sweat and toil of free men." The Assembly agreed its bell should be the largest in all the thirteen colonies. It should ring with a good tone and be engraved with a "brave verse" around the side.

There was, however, a problem. No one in the colonies in 1751 made bells, so Norris unhappily agreed to order the bell from the Whitechapel Foundry in London. The order called for the bell to be twelve feet around at the lip (bottom), and seven and a half feet around at the crown (top). The height from the lip to the crown needed to be three feet, with another two and a half feet of yoke above the crown. The length of the clapper (hammer) inside the bell was to be thirty-eight inches. The cost? About sixty dollars.

It took a year for the bell to arrive, and another year before it was hung in the tower. In 1753 a huge crowd gathered to hear the bell rung for the first time. To the horror of the crowd, the rim of the bell split wide open on the first ring. Norris insisted that the cracked bell not be sent back to England for repairs. He and others were certain the weakness of the bell was a deliberate trick of the British manufacturer though this could not be proved.

John Stow and John Pass were two men with a foundry in Philadelphia, where they made iron molds and cast (formed) iron pieces. However, bells were made of tin and copper, not iron. They took the bell, melted it, added more copper to make it less brittle, and poured it into a new mold. They engraved the verse from the Bible that Norris had originally selected for the bell, they changed the year of the bell's "birth" to 1753, and placed their own names on it as the makers. They also spelled *Pennsylvania* with only one *n—Pensylvania*. This was not a mistake, because at the time this was a common spelling for the colony.

Once again the people gathered to celebrate and hear the chime. Stow pulled the rope, the clapper hit the inside of the bell, and the listeners shuddered. The sound was awful!

Another bell was ordered from Whitechapel Foundry, but before it arrived, Pass and Stowe melted and recast the first bell again. This time they added more tin in hopes of producing the correct sound. The bell was now 70 percent copper and 25 percent tin, with small amounts of lead, zinc, arsenic, nickel, antimony, gold, and silver. Pass and Stow hung this bell in the State House tower in June 1753, and when the clapper rope was pulled, the sound rang out, and nothing cracked. For the next twenty years the bell sounded on many occasions, including each time the Continental Congress delegates (representatives) from all the colonies met.

On July 8, 1776, the bell summoned colonists for the first reading of the **Declaration of Independence**. The declaration announced that the colonies were free and no longer part of Britain or subject to its rules. The people of Philadelphia kept the bell ringing into the night with excitement.

By the fall of 1777, the excitement had turned to fear. The British troops were preparing to march into Philadelphia to use the city as their winter head-quarters. All the bells in Philadelphia's churches and buildings were ordered removed. To keep them from the British, the Great Bell was one of eleven bells loaded onto wagons, covered with hay, and carried to Northampton, where they were hidden in the cellar of the Zion Reformed Church. Wagon drivers John

Jacob Mickley and Frederick Loeser are credited with transporting the bell to safety.

After the British marched out of Philadelphia in 1778, the bell was returned to the State House tower. When it sounded for the death of Supreme Court Chief Justice John Marshall in July 1835, another crack appeared. This was also the year it was first called the Liberty Bell, in an article published by the American Anti-Slavery Society. The writer of the article called its sound "a mockery while one-sixth of the inhabitants are in abject slavery." The bell hung silent for the next ten years before it was mended to ring for a special celebration in honor of George Washington's birthday.

Even with the repair, the bell cracked again. The crack is more than two feet long. In 1853 the bell was removed from the tower, mounted on a stand with thirteen sides representing the thirteen original colonies, and placed on exhibit in the State House. Later the silent bell toured the country by train. Famous composer John Philip Sousa wrote "Liberty Bell March" in celebration of the bell's arrival in Chicago, and this march is often played today by school and community bands. Three coins have been minted with engravings of the Liberty Bell, and three tape recordings of its E-flat strike note are known to exist.

The Liberty Bell is now permanently displayed at Independence National Historic Park in Philadelphia. Each year more than a million people come to Liberty Bell Pavilion to view one of the nation's most treasured symbols of patriotism.

MARGARET COCHRAN CORBIN

FIRST WOMAN WOUNDED ON THE BATTLEFIELD
1751–1800

The first woman to take a soldier's part in the war for liberty.

—From a plaque in New York
honoring Margaret Cochran Corbin

The Congressional Record of the United States contains the names of three women who distinguished themselves for bravery in battle during the Revolutionary War. Margaret Cochran Corbin is one of them. While there were no doubt others who also deserved this recognition, Corbin serves as an example of an extraordinary patriot woman whose capabilities on the battlefield helped win America's independence. At the Battle of Fort Washington on Manhattan Island, New York, she showed that women could do more than cook, clean, wash clothes, and tend to the wounded.

Margaret was born on November 12, 1751, near Chambersburg, Pennsylvania. When she was five, her father, Robert Cochran, was killed by Indians, and her mother was kidnapped. Margaret went to live with her uncle, and in 1772 married John Corbin, a Virginia farmer. Until this time Margaret had lived the life of a typical girl growing up in the colonies. She had no formal schooling and played games such as quoits (horseshoes) and hoop and stick, in which girls threw a hoop from a stick.

Between 1765 and 1774 England passed a series of laws the colonists called the Intolerable Acts. One of these laws forced the Americans to allow British soldiers to live in their homes. Another said British officials could not be tried for crimes committed in the colonies, which allowed them literally to get away with murder. The law that had the most widespread effect was the one that forbade colonists to use the port of Boston. This port was vital to the colonists' ability to trade.

Like other colonists, John and Margaret were angry at the treatment the colonists were receiving. In 1776 John enlisted as a private in the First Company, Pennsylvania Artillery Regiment of the Continental army, and Margaret went with her husband to care for his needs, since each man in the army at that time had to do his own cooking and washing.

John was a cannoneer at Fort Washington, New York. A cannoneer was responsible for keeping the cannon firing during battle. Margaret learned with him how to swab out (clean) the cannon after each firing, how to pour the right amount of powder down the barrel, and how to ram (shove) the six-pound cannonball into place for firing.

Fort Washington was thought to be one of the colonists' strongest forts. It was located on a rocky slope 230 feet above the Hudson River. A large number of Hessian troops (soldiers from Germany paid by the English to fight against the Americans) were stationed southeast of the fort. A small group of American soldiers was stationed outside the main fort to delay any attack that might be made. John Corbin was a cannoneer in this camp, and Margaret was there with him.

On November 16, 1776, as a light snow began to fall, the Hessians attacked. The Americans camped outside fought to keep the Hessians back to give those in the fort time to prepare for battle. Suddenly, the British sprayed a burst of shots over the gunners, and John Corbin and some of his crew fell dead. Others were wounded. Margaret, who had been hiding behind the line, rushed to John but could do nothing to help him. She immediately went into action cleaning, loading, and firing the cannon repeatedly at the approaching enemy line. The Hessians fired back into the small group of fort defenders. Margaret received two shots in her chest and shoulder. One shot nearly ripped off her left arm. Still another hit her cheek.

The commander of Fort Washington was forced to surrender. Some versions of Corbin's life say the British were surprised to find a woman among the wounded prisoners and turned her over to the Americans for care. Others say she was never taken prisoner. Regardless, she was physically disabled for the rest of her life. She also suffered mental disabilities, refusing to bathe and care for herself and hiding from people.

On June 26, 1779, Pennsylvania recognized this heroine for her "distinguished bravery." On July 6, 1779, Congress directed that she receive a military pension. The order said she should be paid "one-half a soldier's monthly pay" and "be given a suit of clothes or the equivalent value in money."

Corbin became known as Captain Molly and lived at West Point with the Invalid Corps until the end of the Revolutionary War. She should not be confused with Molly Pitcher (**Mary Hays McCauley**), another war heroine.

After the war the Invalid Corps at West Point disbanded. No one knows where or how Corbin lived after leaving West Point, though there were occasional reports of her being seen wandering the streets of Philadelphia smoking her pipe.

On January 16, 1800, Margaret Corbin died. She was buried near the Hudson River. A plain stone marked her grave. In 1926 the New York Society of the Daughters of the American Revolution located her grave in a forgotten plot. On April 14, 1926, her remains were removed to the West Point cemetery, where she was reburied with full military honors as the first woman wounded on the battlefield.

JAMES MADISON

CHAMPION FOR THE CONSTITUTION
1751–1836

T was not absent a single day.

—James Madison

On a spring morning in 1802, two men talked intently as they walked in the garden behind the White House. One was well over six feet tall; the other only a few inches past five feet. Several years later **Thomas Jefferson** was asked if he was ever bothered "looking down" upon his most trusted friend, James Madison. Jefferson briskly replied, "I beg to differ, sir. I always looked up to him."

James Madison was born on March 16, 1751, in the home of his grandmother at what is now Port Conway, Virginia. He was the first child of James and Eleanor Conway Madison. He grew up on his father's plantation, Montpelier, in Orange County, Virginia. Like many other plantation children, Madison was taught at home. His grandmother was his first teacher. At about the age of twelve, he was enrolled in a school to learn Greek and Latin, since most colleges would only accept students who could translate those languages into English. Madison could translate both Greek and Latin well by the time he enrolled in the College of New Jersey (now Princeton University). There he studied history, government, and law.

After graduation Madison returned to Montpelier. From 1772 to 1775, he spent most of his time reading and did little else. He was depressed, believing he was not going to live very long. Whatever caused him to imagine he was ill went away as he grew more and more interested in politics. America was preparing to declare independence from Britain, and Madison decided he wanted to be a part of the exciting events taking place. In 1776 he was elected to the Virginia Constitutional Convention, where he met Jefferson. The purpose of the convention was to create a state constitution (a set of rules and laws that tells how a government is organized and run). Madison was very shy, but he and Jefferson soon became close friends and remained so for the rest of their lives.

In 1779 Madison was elected to represent Virginia at the Continental Congress that had been formed to unite the American colonies against the British. Although he had not been present when the **Declaration of Independence** was signed, Madison heartily supported the Revolutionary War.

By the end of the war, Madison had established himself as one of the sharpest young minds in the Continental Congress. He had also fallen in love with Catherine Floyd, and they became engaged. When she broke the engagement, the disappointed Madison again returned to Montpelier, where he spent a lonely winter reading. The more he read, the more he became convinced than the new nation of the United States of America needed a stronger central government than the Articles of Confederation provided. These articles were the rules and laws that the country had been governed by since the end of the war.

From May until September of 1787, Madison was in constant attendance as a delegate at the Constitutional Convention in Philadelphia. The persistent patriot kept a detailed journal of everything that occurred and is credited with ensuring that all the states, regardless of their size, had equal representation under the **Constitution of the United States of America**. He insisted that the Constitution be "the work of many heads and many hands."

Among the powerful opponents to the Constitution were **Patrick Henry** and **George Mason**. They were anti-Federalists who wanted the Constitution to contain a bill of rights to protect the individual freedoms of citizens from the government. Both men left the convention before the Constitution was signed and joined other opponents in writing newspaper articles urging states not to ratify (accept) the Constitution.

Madison teamed with **Alexander Hamilton** and **John Jay** to write a series of pro-Constitution articles published under the pen name **Publius**. Madison is believed to have written at least twenty-eight of the eighty-five articles over the next ten months. The articles became known as *The Federalist Papers* and are still considered to be some of the best articles on political philosophy in the world. It was Madison who led the effort to add the first ten amendments to the Constitution, known as the Bill of Rights, which were adopted by Congress on December 15, 1791, four years after the Constitution was ratified.

In the spring of 1794, Madison met Dolley Todd, a twenty-six-year-old Philadelphia widow. He wrote Jefferson that she had "completely captured" his feelings. Dolley was equally charmed by "the great little Madison." They were married on September 15, 1794, and moved to Montpelier when his term in

Congress ended. They had no children together, but Madison helped raise Dolley's son from her first marriage.

When Jefferson was elected the nation's third president, he asked Madison to be his secretary of state. Madison served in that position from 1801 until the end of Jefferson's second term, then followed Jefferson in 1808 into the White House as the fourth president of the United States. The War of 1812 (1812–1815), fought during his first term, was an unpopular one, often called "Mr. Madison's War" by those who opposed his decision to declare war on Britain. On August 24, 1814, British troops invaded Washington, D.C. and burned the Capitol Building while Madison was away. This and other wartime losses turned many of Madison's friends into foes by the time the Treaty of Ghent was negotiated, ending the war.

Madison was a slaveholder all his life. He argued for the Constitution to abolish (do away with) slavery, but he compromised on the issue rather than risk not getting agreement from all the states on establishing a strong national government. Like some of the other framers (writers), he believed slavery would disappear once the Constitution was firmly in place with its provision prohibiting the future importation of slaves. He served as president of the American Colonization Society, which established the colony of Liberia in Africa for "free persons of color" (African Americans) who wanted to move there.

Madison spent his last years of public service at the University of Virginia. He died on June 28, 1836. He and Dolley, who died in 1849, are buried at Montpelier.

GEORGE ROGERS CLARK

THE "GREAT LONG KNIFE"
1752–1818

*G*reat *things have been affected by a few men . . .*

—General George Rogers Clark

Visitors today to the George Rogers Clark National Historical Park in Vincennes, Indiana, can stand on the site of old Fort Sackville, where the six-foot-tall, two-hundred-pound American frontiersman helped ensure victory for the American colonists in their struggle for independence. Like many, Clark became one of the famous, then for-gotten, patriots.

George Rogers Clark was born on November 19, 1752, the second son of John and Ann Rogers Clark. The Clarks were rural Virginia landowners, and George's early education included learning to hunt, fish, and trap. When he was eleven, he and his older brother went to live with their grandfather so that they could attend a private school. Rugged and taller than any of his classmates, George was restless inside the classroom. He stayed in school for only a few months before deciding to learn surveying from his grandfather. A surveyor prepares maps and descriptions of land.

When George was eighteen, his brother William was born. William later became famous leading the Corps of Discovery expedition to explore the territory gained in the Louisiana Purchase with Meriwether Lewis.

Fame was not what George Clark went looking for when he headed west on a surveying trip into the Kentucky wilderness. Like many other young Americans, he wanted to claim land and settle there. He soon earned a reputation as a superb wilderness fighter and a backwoods leader who could inspire men with his strength, thinking skills, and speaking abilities. In June 1776 the people of Kentucky elected him their spokesman to seek help from Virginia's governor, **Patrick Henry**, for protection of their settlements. What Clark actually did was convince Governor Henry to authorize him to raise an army to capture the Northwest Territories for the United States. This wilderness area included what is now Ohio, Indiana, Illinois, Wisconsin, Michigan, and parts of Minnesota.

Clark secretly gathered a group of men armed with long-barreled rifles, and in 1778 they began their travels down the Ohio River. He trained his troops at Corn Island and then launched a successful campaign capturing British posts on the Mississippi River and the Wabash River, at times without firing a shot. Part of Clark's shrewd strategy included gathering leaders from fifteen western Indian tribes and asking them to form an alliance against their mutual enemy, the British. Because Clark showed them so much respect, the Indian leaders pledged their support against the British.

Lieutenant Governor Henry Hamilton recaptured the post on the Wabash River for the British, but Clark did not give up. In a plan considered one of the boldest in American military history, he took 172 men on foot across 240 miles of flooded, frozen rivers and plains to recapture the post. During their seventeen-day march, the men waded in icy water up to their necks and had to chew the bark of trees to keep from starving. Almost half of them suffered from chills and fever. Arriving at the fort at dusk, the outnumbered riflemen kept up their deadly firing all night to confuse the British, and Hamilton surrendered to Clark the next day.

Clark continued to fight on the frontier until 1783, when he was given the job as Virginia's surveyor of public lands. When Clark applied to the government of Virginia for wages for the five years he and his men had fought without being paid, the government told him they would have to have receipts for all of the expenses he had paid with his own money to remove the British from the Northwest Territories. Clark shipped a large box with all of his receipts to the Virginia Statehouse. He waited, but the money never came. The people to whom he owed money did come, however. They sued Clark and won, forcing him to give them the land he had been granted for military service to pay their claims.

For the next thirty years Clark, who never married, did not have a home of his own. He finally built a two-room log cabin on a hill overlooking the falls of the Ohio River. He lived in poverty, relying on his hunting and fishing skills to survive. The old Indian leaders who had given him the honorary name "the Great Long Knife" sometimes came to visit. Other visitors came only to inquire about his famous brother, William, who had relied on his brother's vast knowledge of the frontier to make his Corps of Discovery expedition.

Clark suffered a stroke in 1809. He fell into a fire and burned his leg so badly that it had to be amputated. There was no anesthetic to put him to sleep, so Clark asked that "two fifers and two drummers play the commands" while the doctors performed the operation. **Fifers and drummers** were military musicians who played flutes and drums to announce commands in battle.

On a winter day in 1812, a messenger arrived at the home of Clark's sister, with whom he was living in Locust Grove near Louisville, Kentucky. The messenger said that the State of Virginia had agreed to begin paying Clark four hundred dollars a month in appreciation for his past services. The messenger also laid a beautifully engraved sword across Clark's chair, but the long-forgotten patriot could not pick it up. The hand he had used to help win the Northwest Territories for the United States had been paralyzed by another stroke.

Clark died on February 13, 1818. According to historian Walter Havinhurst, almost a century later, in 1913, a large box of moldy papers was discovered in the attic of the Virginia Statehouse. Inside were hundreds of handwritten pieces of paper showing how much Clark had paid for salt, nails, candles, shirts, rifles, flour, and even Indian interpreters. The box had somehow been misplaced after arriving at the statehouse and had never been opened. It was simply marked "G. Clark: Unpaid."

BETSY ROSS

THE WOMAN BEHIND THE LEGEND OF THE STARS AND STRIPES
1752–1836

Would that it were true.

Before there was a United States of America, flags of various designs were used to identify the colonies, ships, and militias (citizen soldiers). Most vexillologists (flag experts) say evidence is lacking to prove the claims made by William Canby that his grandmother, Betsy Ross, created the Stars and Stripes at the personal request of

General **George Washington**. Canby first told this story in 1870 to the Historical Society of Pennsylvania. It became so popular that it was accepted as the truth.

While Canby's story was largely fiction, there really was a Betsy Ross. She was born on January 1, 1752, as Elizabeth Griscom, the eighth of seventeen children. Her parents were devout Quakers from Philadelphia. Her father was a successful carpenter, as were his father and grandfather before him. Though many girls did not go to school during this time, Betsy attended Quaker schools, where she studied reading and writing and learned a skill she could use to earn money.

When she finished her formal schooling, Betsy became an apprentice upholsterer, learning to make coverings for furniture, saddles, carriages, and other items. In addition to upholstery, Betsy became well known for making colors (flags) for sailors to fly on their ships.

Betsy met another apprentice upholsterer, John Ross, who was a member of the Episcopal Church. Betsy's family did not want her to marry a man who was not a Quaker, so in November 1773 she and John eloped across the Delaware River into New Jersey and were married in Hugg's Tavern. Her family refused to have any further communication with Betsy after she married John.

Betsy began a different life with her husband. She attended Christ Church. General Washington sometimes occupied the pew next to hers, so it is possible that Betsy sewed for Washington. Betsy and John set up their own upholstery business in 1775, but the increasing problems between the British and the colonists hurt their business. Fabrics and other supplies were in short supply. People who had once been their customers were no longer able to afford their services.

On January 1, 1776, General George Washington ordered the Grand Union flag to be raised above his headquarters to show support for the Continental army. However, the Grand Union flag looked very much like the British "Union

Jack" flag. Confusion followed. When Washington learned that the British thought the flag was the sign of surrender by the Americans, he knew that a new flag for America had to be designed.

Several days later an explosion at an ammunition warehouse severely injured John, who had joined the militia and was on guard duty. He died on January 21, 1776.

According to Canby, three representatives from the Continental Congress secretly visited his grandmother in May 1776. America had not yet declared independence, but Canby said these representatives—George Washington, **Robert Morris**, and John's uncle, George Ross—came to discuss having a flag made for America that would represent the union of the colonies. No mention, however, of such a committee or meeting has been documented in any private journal of these men or in government records.

According to Canby, Washington gave Betsy a sketch of a design for a flag containing stars with six points. Betsy preferred a five-pointed star. She supposedly folded a piece of paper and cut a star with one snip to show the men how cleverly she could make the five-pointed stars. Washington reportedly redrew the flag using the five-pointed stars and gave her the job of making the new American flag. She sewed it with seven red stripes and six white stripes representing the thirteen colonies. Also representing the colonies were thirteen white, five-pointed stars, arranged in a circle on a blue field.

The circle design is one of the reasons historians do not believe Canby's story to be completely accurate. They say an artist, Charles Weisgerber, actually created the circle design as he painted a picture of his idea of what happened as Ross made the flag.

Whether or not she made the flag as her family claimed, Ross was a dedicated patriot. She joined the Free (Fighting) Quakers, who supported the fight for America's independence. British soldiers took over her home when they took control of Philadelphia, and while Ross was required to use her needlework skills to sew British uniforms, she secretly made pouches to hold gunpowder for the Continental army.

Ross married again in 1777. Her husband, Joseph Ashburn, was a sea captain. They had two daughters before Ashburn was captured by the British. He died in March 1782 while imprisoned in England.

In May 1783 Betsy married for the third time. This husband, John Claypoole, had been captured and imprisoned at the same prison as Ashburn. Betsy and John had five daughters. He died in 1817 after a long illness, and she continued her work in the upholstery shop until 1827.

Betsy Ross Ashburn Claypoole died on January 30, 1836, and was buried in the Free Quakers Burial Ground in Philadelphia. She is now buried in the court-yard adjacent to the Betsy Ross House, also in Philadelphia.

On June 14, 1777, the Continental Congress adopted the national flag. The resolution said: "Resolved: that the flag of the United States be thirteen stripes, alternate red and white; that the union be thirteen stars, white in a blue field, representing a new constellation." Doubt remains as to who first designed the flag officially adopted by Congress. There can be no doubt, however, that Betsy Ross is a symbol of the patriotic women who were part of America's struggle for independence.

JACK JOUETT

THE OTHER MIDNIGHT RIDER
1754–1822

But for Captain Jack Jouett's heroic ride, the Revolutionists would have been only unsuccessful rebels.

—Stuart G. Gibboney,
president of the Thomas Jefferson
Memorial Foundation, 1926

Unlike **Paul Revere**, whose midnight ride in 1775 was made famous by the poet Henry Wadsworth Longfellow, Captain Jack Jouett is unknown to most Americans. Yet some historians believe that Jouett's midnight ride was equally heroic.

Jouett had no intention of being a hero the evening of June 3, 1781. He was enjoying the company of friends at Cuckoo Tavern in Louisa County, Virginia. A tavern during the Revolutionary War was much like a modern-day motel and restaurant, where people gathered to eat, socialize, conduct business, and rest from their travels. On leave from the Virginia militia (citizen soldiers), Jouett had come home to Louisa County, where he was born in 1754, to help his father arrange to get more supplies for the Continental army.

Jouett relaxed on the lawn of the tavern. His horse, Sallie, grazed nearby. Had there been motion pictures in 1781, Jouett would have been a leading man. Handsome and six feet, four inches tall, he was known as an accomplished horseman. Sallie was a thoroughbred, a horse born to run. Jouett and Sallie were soon to prove their skills on a daring ride the British enemy had not considered possible.

In the quiet of the late evening, Jouett awakened to the hoofbeats of nearly two hundred galloping horses. A glimpse of the approaching dragoons (mounted soldiers) sent shivers up Jouett's back. They were the troops of none other than British colonel Banastre Tarleton, better known as "the Butcher."

Jouett knew Tarleton could have only one objective that night. The Virginia General Assembly, led by Governor **Thomas Jefferson**, was meeting in Charlottesville after escaping from Richmond. Tarleton intended to storm Charlottesville and capture Jefferson, **Patrick Henry**, **Richard Henry Lee**, and the other members of the assembly. The militia did not have enough men or equipment to fight the British dragoons. Most of the trained fighting men were in the north with General **Washington**.

Unless Jouett could get to Charlottesville before the dragoons, Jefferson, Henry, Lee, and all the others helping to lead the rebellion against British rule in the American colonies would be captured and most certainly killed. Knowing that Tarleton's troops filled the main road to Charlottesville, Jouett mounted his horse and charged into the dense woods to ride the forty miles to Charlottesville through tangled trees, sharp brush, and treacherous gullies. A full moon helped him pick a path, but it also made him an easier target if some of Tarleton's men were hiding in the woods. Jouett knew his life would end at their swords if they caught him, but he never considered turning back.

The thick underbrush tore at Sallie's legs. Tree limbs cut deep into Jouett's face. Ignoring the pain and the blood, Jouett urged Sallie on. A portrait of Jouett painted later in his life shows the permanent scars from the brutal cuts he received to his face as he rode through the night.

A well-conditioned horse can gallop for long periods of time without getting tired. Sallie was in good shape, and with Jouett's skill as a rider, she was able to continue galloping without stopping to rest. They arrived before dawn at Monticello, Governor Jefferson's home near Charlottesville. Jouett woke Jefferson, crying, "You must leave immediately to escape the Butcher!" Then he rode on to Charlottesville to warn the rest of the legislators.

Jefferson hurried his family away from Monticello, gathered all his important papers, and left. Minutes later, he realized he had dropped his walking sword in his haste, and he headed back to Monticello to get it. He barely got away on his horse before the British entered the house.

After the war Jouett moved to Harrodsburg, the first settlement in Kentucky. He married Sally Robards and became known for raising excellent cattle and horses. He worked to help Kentucky gain statehood in 1792.

He died at his daughter's home on March 1, 1822. Schools and ships have been named in Jouett's honor, but no great poet has ever written an epic poem about his midnight ride. As much as Jouett cherished the silver-mounted pistols and the jeweled sword presented to him by the Virginia Assembly for his heroic deed, he said his greatest honor was in saving the lives of men who lived to became more famous than he.

MARY HAYS McCAULEY

MOLLY PITCHER
C. 1754–1832

From the ranks this woman came, by the cannon won her fame; 'Tis true she could not write her name, but freedom's hand hath carved it.

— From a poem by Sarah Woods Parkinson engraved on the monument honoring Mary Hays McCauley in Carlisle, Pennsylvania

Mary Hays ran back and forth in the sweltering heat, carrying her bucket between the small stream and the battlefield of Monmouth, New Jersey.

"Molly, the pitcher!" The American soldiers pleaded with her to bring them water for their thirst and to cool the cannons. Suddenly, Mary saw her husband, William, fall to the ground beside the cannon where he served. Mary threw down her bucket and grabbed the rammer staff to keep the cannon firing. No longer was she "Molly Pitcher," carrying water to soldiers. She was a gunner fighting for independence.

No one knows the date Mary was born, but historians believe it was around 1754. Some early accounts said she was of Irish descent. Others said she was German, and her maiden name was Ludwig. Another version says she was the daughter of a New Jersey dairy farmer. All accounts describe her as a large, plain woman whose speech could sometimes be anything but ladylike. She could not read or write, so all the written information about her came from other people, which is why many of the stories of her heroism include different details. She is often confused with another Revolutionary War heroine, **Margaret Cochran Corbin**.

According to most historians, the fields near the Monmouth Courthouse rocked with musket and cannon fire on June 28, 1778. The British redcoats, dressed in their scarlet woolen jackets even in the heat, were slowly advancing on the Americans. General **George Washington** arrived to rally his army after they had fled in all directions under the poor leadership of General Charles Lee. In the two years since the **Declaration of Independence** had been signed, the Americans had suffered many losses. Until Washington arrived at Monmouth, this battle appeared to be yet another disaster in the making for the patriots.

It was not unusual for the wives of soldiers to be near a battlefield. While General Washington did not like having the wives and sometimes even the children of the soldiers nearby, the cooking and laundry duties they performed were helpful. Some soldiers referred to any woman in the camp as "Molly." The women often learned to perform the same duties as their husbands. Six men were required to operate a cannon, and Mary Hays had no doubt learned the firing sequence perfectly: Charge the piece! Ram down the charge! Run out the piece! Take aim! Pick! Prime! Make ready! Give! Fire!

It is unknown how long Mary continued to take William's place at the cannon. After the Americans succeeded in defeating the British, the men who had fought beside her told stories about her heroic actions. One man said he saw her carry a wounded soldier off the field on her shoulders. Joseph Martin, a soldier close to her during the fight, said a British shot went directly between her legs and

Mary Hays McCauley takes to a cannon during the War of Independence

ripped off the lower part of her muslin skirt. Without moving from her position, Mary kept helping fire the cannon. Various artists later depicted these accounts, adding their own interpretations in paintings that appeared in history texts.

Mary did not continue to fight as a soldier. While William recovered, she served as a nurse with the Fourth Continental Artillery Regiment. She could be seen wearing brogans (heavy boots) and a ruffled white cap, tending to the wounded and carrying the dead from the battlefields.

After the war Mary and William returned to Carlisle, Pennsylvania, where he died. Mary later married John McCauley. After he died in 1813, she worked as a housekeeper in the statehouse at Carlisle and as a caretaker for invalids. In 1822 the Pennsylvania legislature unanimously awarded Mary a yearly pension of forty dollars for her "services rendered in the Revolutionary War."

On June 28, 1916, Pennsylvania placed a monument near what is believed to be Mary's grave at Carlisle. They put a life-size statue of Mary holding a rammer staff, and the sculptor used the facial features from five of her great-grandchildren to sculpt her face.

The Congressional Record of the United States contains the names of three women who distinguished themselves in battle during the Revolutionary War. Mary Hays McCauley is one of them.

DR. JAMES THACHER

SURGEON, SOLDIER, SCRIBE
1754–1844

an we set our feet on their rock without swearing, by the spirit of our fathers, to defend it and our country?

—Dr. James Thacher

In 1775 twenty-one-year-old Dr. James Thacher set off to join the Continental army. Along with his bag of surgeon's tools, he took with him his quill pens, a small bottle of ink, and a supply of blank paper he kept folded in a leather pouch. As he passed through Plymouth, Massachusetts, he stopped in the town square in front of a large rock. The rock had been moved into town from the waterfront. It was said to be the very rock the Pilgrims had first stepped on when they arrived in America.

Thacher scribbled his feelings of patriotism on the paper in his pouch before hurrying to Cambridge, Massachusetts. By the time the Revolutionary War ended, his pouch would bulge with hundreds of pieces of paper detailing his life as a surgeon and a soldier for the patriot cause.

James Thacher was born in 1754. His father was a farmer on Cape Cod. When James was sixteen, he became an apprentice (someone who worked with a person to learn a skill) to Abner Hersey, a well-known doctor from Barnstable, Massachusetts. There were about three thousand doctors in America at this time, and very few of them had gone to a medical school for training. Thacher considered himself very fortunate to have the opportunity to study with Hersey, because Hersey actually had a few medical books.

Thacher joined the Continental army at Cambridge, near Boston, as a surgeon's mate earning $18 a month. When he became a full regimental surgeon, his salary doubled.

When a smallpox epidemic raged through Boston in the summer of 1776, Thacher became ill and was left behind to care for other sick soldiers. The deadly disease did not frighten Thacher as much as seeing the horrors experienced by the soldiers wounded on the battlefields. In his journal he described the terrible condition of the hospitals, which were usually churches or homes where the wounded were taken. After the battle at Fort Ticonderoga, New York, in 1777, he helped perform many amputations on soldiers without anesthetic. Many soldiers died because the surgeons had no way to stop bleeding or control infections in the unsanitary facilities.

Thacher wrote detailed descriptions of each day's events: the men, medical treatments, battles, weather conditions, and day-to-day life in the camps. His journal included a complete description of the *Turtle*, the first submarine used by the Americans in war.

Although his service as a surgeon was important, Thacher wanted to do more than tend to wounds. He joined the First Virginia Regiment as a soldier, fighting as well as caring for the wounded. He then served with the First Massachusetts Regiment doing dangerous patrols ahead of the main army. He was at the Battle of Yorktown in New York and was present when British general Charles Cornwallis surrendered to General **George Washington**.

At the end of the war, Thacher resigned from the army. He had little in the way of personal goods to show for his service, but he had gained a wealth of experience. He returned to Plymouth to practice medicine and teach medical students, using his journal in which he had often written in the dark of night on the battlefield as his textbook.

Thacher married Susannah Hayward of Bridgewater, Massachusetts, and they had six children. Only two daughters lived to be adults. In many of the letters he wrote to his daughters, he offered practical medical advice for "avoiding fevers" and urged them to remember "the daughters of our revolutionary fathers who are no more." He began writing articles on various diseases, including "Observations on Hydrophobia" (rabies), which was published in 1812. These articles added to his reputation as both a doctor and a scholar with honorary degrees from Harvard and Dartmouth colleges.

In 1820 Thacher became a founding member of the Pilgrim Society, an organization dedicated to recording American history. As the society's "cabinet-keeper" (librarian), he began a collection of historical writing about the Pilgrims and early America.

Thacher began to lose his hearing about this time. Deafness forced him to end his medical practice and teaching, but it allowed him to focus on what may be his greatest patriotic contribution to the nation. In 1823 he published *Thacher's Military Journal During the American Revolutionary War*. The book was his eyewitness account of the Revolutionary War taken from the pages of his journal. It is still considered one of the most factually accurate books written about the Revolutionary period of American history. Included are personal experiences Thacher had with George Washington, **Baron Friedrich von Steuben, Marquis de Lafayette**, and other patriot leaders.

Thacher's *American Medical Biography*, published four years later, was the first book to list information about every doctor in America. Medicine was not the only subject he wrote about in his "silent" years. He published articles and books about fruit trees, apple cider, bees, and ghost stories.

The rock that inspired James Thacher's patriotic devotion as a teenager was moved to the front lawn of the Pilgrim Society in 1834. He died at his nearby home ten years later at the age of ninety.

NATHAN HALE

SCHOOLTEACHER SPY
1755–1776

I regret that I have only one life to lose for my country.

—One of several versions of Nathan Hale's last words before being hanged by the British as a spy

He was a schoolteacher who never owned property, never married, and failed in his final mission as a spy for **George Washington**. Yet Nathan Hale is remembered as one of the outstanding patriots of the Revolutionary War.

Hale was born on June 6, 1755, in Coventry, Connecticut, the sixth of twelve children, to Richard and

Elizabeth Strong Hale. At age fourteen Nathan went to Yale College. He graduated with high honors in 1773.

A school in East Haddam, Connecticut, hired Hale, but he soon moved to New London, Connecticut, to teach. Unlike many other people during this period, he believed women should receive an education just like men. In 1774 he taught a class of twenty young women from five o'clock to seven o'clock every morning, and the rest of the day he taught young men.

Hale was a good teacher, but he wanted to be a soldier and fight for independence from the British. In July 1775 he joined the local militia (citizen soldiers), saying, "Let us never lay down our arms until we gain independence."

Hale's militia took part in a battle to free Boston from the control of the British. Then they joined General George Washington's army to defend New York. The successful raid planned by Hale on a British frigate (armed warship), the *Phoenix,* brought the young captain recognition and a transfer to a special regiment that became known as Knowlton's Rangers. Washington, in desperate need of spies who could provide information about British positions and movements, had Knowlton ask for volunteers to spy on the British. In those days spying was a dishonorable job considered unworthy of a gentleman. Gentleman or not, anyone caught spying would be punished by hanging.

Hale was the only man to volunteer. He disguised himself as a Dutch schoolmaster, wearing a plain brown suit and a round, broad-brimmed hat. He took his college diploma in case someone should question his claim of being a schoolmaster.

Hale left his camp at Harlem Heights, New York, on September 12 and journeyed to Norwalk, Connecticut. He found a boat to take him across Long Island Sound and landed close to Huntington Bay. "Come back for me on September 20," he told the boatman. He planned to move west, behind British lines, then retrace his steps to meet the boatman a week later to report to General Washington the British activities.

Hale slipped into New York, where he found that the British had already taken most of Manhattan. Washington was entrenched behind the bluffs at Harlem Heights. Hale stayed in New York City, taking notes on British troop locations and making sketches of British fortifications.

Hale started back through British lines on September 20, hoping the boatman would be waiting. British soldiers, suspecting he was a spy, captured him on September 21, and searched him before he reached Huntington Bay. They found his papers, full of details about their locations and written in Latin, hidden in the soles of his shoes.

When British General Howe questioned him about the papers, Hale told them his name and rank and admitted to being a spy for General Washington. Howe ordered that Hale be hanged without a trial the next morning.

Hale spent the night of September 21 at Howe's headquarters. He asked for a Bible and a minister, but the British refused. Still, they were impressed by his confidence and willingness to die honorably.

The next morning, while the British made plans to hang him, Hale asked for writing materials to write to his mother and a fellow soldier. British Provost-major Cunningham destroyed both letters because he did not want the Americans to "know they had a man in their army who could die with so much firmness."

At about eleven o'clock the morning of September 22, the British hanged Hale from an apple tree in Rutger's Orchard, near what is today the intersection of East Broadway and Market Street in New York City. The British left him hanging there for three days as an example to the rebels before they cut him down and buried him in an unmarked grave.

During the next several years various people reported that just before he died, Hale said, "I regret that I have but one life to lose for my country." Other versions have him saying, "one life to give for my country" or, "I regret that I have not more lives than one to offer in [America's] service."

What Hale's exact words were is not as important as what he did. He considered no job dishonorable if his country needed it done, and he volunteered to serve when others refused. He is considered the first American to be captured and executed as a spy. Stories of his bravery in life and death inspired other Americans in their fight for freedom during and since the Revolution.

ALEXANDER HAMILTON

SOLDIER AND STATESMAN
1755–1804

I am quite willing to take on the task.

—Alexander Hamilton

Look at Alexander Hamilton's picture on a ten-dollar bill. His face and clothes suggest that he led the life of a gentleman. It is easy to see him as the brave soldier and brilliant statesman who created our monetary system and helped design a government that made

America great. What cannot be seen is the shadow of painful sacrifice this great patriot made in his service to America.

Hamilton was born on the British West Indies island of Nevis. His father abandoned the family, and Alexander lived in poverty. When he was thirteen years old, Alexander's mother died, and his life took a dramatic turn. A local clergyman raised funds to send him to the American colonies in 1772. He attended King's College, now known as Columbia University.

The hardships of his early life fired Hamilton's patriotic love for his new homeland of America. During the Revolutionary War his high-level thinking skills quickly made him a leader. Two years after he joined the New York militia (citizen soldiers) in 1775, General **George Washington** named him an aide-de-camp (assistant), with the rank of lieutenant colonel. This gave Hamilton access to important people and set the stage for his future in politics.

Most important, it gave Hamilton a chance to voice his strong opinions. He did not hesitate to speak against the economic and political troubles that got in the way of the American army's ability to fight the war.

By the end of the Revolutionary War, Hamilton had earned a reputation as a man of unusual intelligence. His outspoken ways had also created many enemies. He shifted his efforts away from fighting on the battlefield to fighting with his writing and speaking skills. Hamilton wanted a stronger central government for the new nation. This did not appeal to many Americans, who had just come through the War of Independence.

By 1787 the United States was deeply in debt, and Congress was unable to impose taxes to get the country out of financial trouble. The states began raising tariffs (charges) against each other, hurting trade and creating all kinds of havoc. The nation was just beginning, and already a war among its citizens threatened its existence.

Against this stormy background Hamilton stepped forward with a call for a constitutional convention. A constitution is a written document establishing the principles and methods by which a nation is governed. Until this time the United States had been loosely held together by the Articles of Confederation, adopted in 1781 as the first constitution for the United States. They did not provide for a strong central government. Hamilton realized that if the country was to survive, it must have a central government with the power to handle national problems.

When the convention met, some of Hamilton's more extreme views disturbed the other delegates (representatives) who had agreed to meet. He felt the country should be governed by "a talented few" and that most people were too selfish or too ignorant to be trusted in positions of power. Most of the other delegates at the convention rejected this view.

"The choice is between this government with some promise of success and no national government at all," Hamilton told the other delegates when he asked

Meeting of the Constitutional Convention

to sign his name to the **Constitution of the United States of America**. He was the only delegate from New York to do so.

Hamilton's devotion to the United States was stronger than his disappointment that the proposed Constitution was not what he had wanted it to be. The man often described as "charming" even by his enemies immediately began using his charm and his talents to persuade each state to ratify (agree to abide by) the Constitution.

Along with **James Madison** and **John Jay**, Hamilton authored *The Federalist Papers*, a collection of eighty-five essays written secretly over a period of ten months under the pen name **Publius**. These essays are credited with convincing people to vote to accept the Constitution. In a letter to a friend, Hamilton wrote that he had "sacrificed more than anyone for the Constitution."

During the early 1790s Hamilton feuded with Secretary of State **Thomas Jefferson**. Hamilton wanted to persuade President Washington to favor close ties with England, but Jefferson favored France. Hamilton interfered with Jefferson's foreign policy efforts by warning the English representatives that Jefferson favored France. He asked them to work with him or directly with the president to advance their interests. Hamilton went so far as to convince the president to send John Jay to England to negotiate a treaty, a direct interference with Jefferson's duties. Not surprisingly, Jefferson resented this interference and resigned.

President Washington appointed Hamilton as the nation's first secretary of the treasury. It was in this role that he made some of his most important and lasting contributions to our nation. His vision of every state in the nation using the same currency (money) has survived to the present day. Yet, in pressing for these ideas, Hamilton suffered vicious attacks against his character and his beliefs. He was even accused of fraud (cheating). This charge was never proved.

In the face of opposition, Hamilton didn't back down. He faced his enemies head-on. Hamilton had a bitter dispute with Aaron Burr, who was elected vice president in 1800. Hamilton wrote an article in which he said he looked upon

Burr as "a dangerous man, one who ought not to be trusted with the reins of government."

Burr took these words as the worst of insults. In those days it was acceptable to settle such quarrels by a duel (an arranged combat in which two people fought with deadly weapons). Burr insisted on having a pistol duel with Hamilton. This challenge placed Hamilton in a terrible position. His son, Philip, had died in a duel three years earlier, and Hamilton hated the practice. In a letter to his wife, Elizabeth, he wrote that his Christian belief made him "determined to risk his own life rather than take the life of another."

Hamilton agreed to meet Burr in battle on July 11, 1804, in Weehawken, New Jersey, but planned to withhold his fire, hoping to give Burr a chance to reconsider. Burr, however, did not hesitate. His bullet hit Hamilton in the stomach and lodged in his spine. Hamilton was rushed to a friend's house, where he died the next day. He is buried in Trinity Churchyard in New York City.

Alexander Hamilton often said of himself that he was a failure. Time has proven he was an outstanding success as a devoted patriot of the United States of America.

JOHN TRUMBULL

ARTIST OF THE REVOLUTION
1756–1843

The greatest motive I had for continuing my pursuit of painting has been to commemorate the great events of our country's Revolution.

—John Trumbull, in a letter to Thomas Jefferson

Fifteen-year-old John Trumbull knew it was useless to argue. His father wanted him to go to Harvard and study for the ministry or law. John wanted to do neither. He would go to Harvard to please his father, he told himself, but once there he would study art. Perhaps, someday, he would create a painting that would make his patriotic father proud.

The youngest of six children, John Trumbull was born on June 6, 1756, in Lebanon, Connecticut. His father, Jonathan, had served as a soldier and was a colonial governor of Connecticut. His mother, Faith Robinson Trumbull, was a descendant of the *Mayflower* Pilgrims. Both parents were dedicated to America's independence.

John was often ill as a child, and when he was five he fell, severely damaging the sight in his left eye. The injury did not keep him from developing his skills as an artist or becoming a brilliant student. He entered Harvard as a fifteen-year-old junior in 1772 and graduated the next year as the youngest in his class.

Trumbull spent time after he graduated copying art masterpieces he saw in Boston studios. He was seriously determined to become a professional painter, regardless of his father's wishes. However, when it became clear America was headed for war with Britain, he put art out of his mind to join the colonists in their fight for independence.

Trumbull raised a militia (citizen soldiers) among Harvard students and then signed on to the First Connecticut Regiment as an assistant to a commanding officer. On July 27, 1775, he became an aide to General **George Washington**. This experience resulted in Trumbull's lifelong fascination with Washington. He idolized him. He would eventually paint thirty-four portraits of Washington, providing future generations with some of the most accurate depictions of Washington recorded.

Trumbull's association with Washington gave him the opportunity to become acquainted with many of America's leading patriots. After his military service, Trumbull set out for Paris, where he met **Benjamin Franklin, John Adams**, and Adams's fourteen-year old son, **John Quincy Adams**. Armed with letters of introduction from Franklin, he went to England to study with the English artist Benjamin West, who painted historic works. West was impressed by Trumbull's skills. He told Trumbull, "I have no hesitation to say that nature intended you for a painter."

Trumbull decided to devote his career to keeping alive the memory of the American Revolution through art. He was imprisoned for a while in England, accused of being a traitor for helping America rebel. For several years he earned very little money painting. He once told another artist, "I would have been a beggar had I relied wholly on paintings for my support."

When Trumbull returned to America, his parents still did not think being an artist—even a patriotic artist—was an honorable profession. John told his father, "I intend to depict the birth of our new nation." For the next sixteen years he did exactly that.

Trumbull's paintings can generally be divided into two major types: portraits

John Trumbull's The Death of General Warren at the Battle of Bunker's Hill

of people, and heroic scenes of the American Revolution. One painting, *The Battle of Bunker's Hill*, which now hangs in an art gallery at Yale University, depicts a number of soldiers in close combat. The dramatic painting shows a soldier dying in the arms of a comrade. **Thomas Jefferson** and John Adams were so impressed by this painting that they began to advise Trumbull about events they hoped he would paint. They shared his belief that the story of America's sacrifices for independence needed to be preserved in pictures for future generations.

Not all of Trumbull's paintings, however, were of the battles of the Revolutionary War. One of his most famous paintings is of the signing of the **Declaration of Independence**. Trumbull insisted each of his paintings be as accurate as possible, and this one was no exception. He spent more than thirty years working on it. He traveled from Paris to England and throughout the United States carrying his small canvas to paint portraits of the thirty-six living delegates. To picture those who had died, he gathered information from their friends and family and from other reliable portraits. Some he painted from his own personal memory. Trumbull painted a portrait of Benjamin Harrison by looking at Harrison's son.

When he was thirty-three, Trumbull fell in love with Harriet Wadsworth, who rejected him. He became involved with another woman, by whom he had a son. When he was forty-four, he married Sarah Hope Harvey of London. His painting of her depicts the beautiful woman he loved until her death in 1824. That same year he completed reproducing four of his most famous paintings for the U.S. Capitol's rotunda, the room beneath the Capitol dome. President **James Madison** selected the rotunda paintings, among them a replica of Trumbull's original painting of the Declaration of Independence. Trumbull earned $32,000 for eight years of work on the project.

For the remaining years of his life, Trumbull's art was not in step with the attitudes and interests of Americans. After the War of 1812 (1812–1815), the American people wanted to put their wartime past behind them. Many felt

Trumbull's work glorified war and the wealthy, and that his painting skills had diminished due to age and eyesight problems.

Had it not been for John Trumbull, much of the visual history of the Revolutionary War period would not exist. When he was seventy-five, he donated his personal art collection to Yale University in exchange for a lifetime income of one thousand dollars a year. He lived another twelve years. His paintings can also be seen at the Metropolitan Museum of Art in New York; the National Gallery of Art, the Smithsonian in Washington, D.C., and other museums around the world.

Trumbull died on November 10, 1843. He is buried beside Sarah in a tomb built beneath the art gallery at Yale. His most famous, full-length portrait of George Washington hangs above the tomb near an inscription that summarizes Trumbull's life: "To his Country he gave his SWORD and PENCIL."

MARQUIS DE LAFAYETTE

FRENCH HERO OF THE AMERICAN
REVOLUTION
1757–1834

*Serving America is to my heart
an inexpressible happiness.*

—Marquis de Lafayette

His friends described the Marquis de
Lafayette as a man "so handsome he
should be a statue." His enemies were
awed by his charm as much as they
feared his skills as a soldier. Others of
his social class in Paris considered him
a traitor for his devotion to individual
freedoms. Americans remember him

as a reckless teenager who gave up a life of luxury to fight for America's independence.

The Marquis de Lafayette's given name was Marie Joseph Paul Yves Roch Gilbert du Motier. *Marquis* is a title given to French noblemen, and *Lafayette* identified his family's land grants in France. He is usually referred to as simply Lafayette. He was born on September 6, 1757, in Chavaniac, France. His birthplace was later renamed Chavaniac-Lafayette.

Lafayette's father died while a soldier for France when Lafayette was two years old. His mother died when he was twelve. He entered the French army when he was only fourteen, and at sixteen he married Marie Adrienne Françoise de Noailles. She was from one of the wealthiest families in France.

In 1775 Lafayette met the duke of Gloucester, the younger brother of King George III, at a meeting of the Masonic fraternal order. The duke was a foe of his brother's policies with America. He sympathized with the Americans' desire for independence and encouraged Lafayette to go to America as a volunteer soldier "for the people fighting for liberty."

Despite the objections of his wife's family, Lafayette eagerly accepted from an American diplomat in France a commission as a major general in the Continental army. When Lafayette left for America, he left his lifestyle of wealth and privilege behind.

Lafayette arrived near Charleston, South Carolina, on June 13, 1777, bringing several other French officers with him. He headed to Philadelphia and was accepted by the Continental Congress as a volunteer who agreed to serve without pay. A short time later he met and became a lifelong friend to General **George Washington**. Lafayette became a member of Washington's staff and was wounded at the Battle of Brandywine in Pennsylvania, in September 1777. He rejoined Washington's forces after he recovered from his wounds.

Lafayette remained loyal to Washington when a group of officers tried to have Washington removed as the commander of the troops at Valley Forge,

Pennsylvania. These officers did not like Washington and resented his confidence in Lafayette. General Horatio Gates, one of the officers who wanted Washington removed, later convinced several members of Congress to allow him to develop a campaign to invade Canada. He designated Lafayette to lead the invasion. Lafayette knew such a plan would be a disaster and did not want to accept the command. Washington convinced him to accept, assuring Lafayette that the expedition would never be carried out.

Lafayette went to Albany, New York, expecting the order to invade Canada to go forward. He found a small force of about 1,200 ill-prepared, ill-clothed, ill-fed, and unpaid soldiers who were outraged that Congress would order them to attempt an invasion in midwinter. Lafayette's dramatic writing skills produced a report on the situation that convinced Congress to delay the invasion. Just as Washington predicted, the invasion of Canada never occurred.

Lafayette returned to Valley Forge in April 1778. Along with General **Nathanael Greene**, he aided in the battles in Rhode Island and was credited with saving one thousand men and their supplies from being captured by the British. When it appeared the American armies were in control, Lafayette formally requested permission to return to France to visit his family.

Back in France, Lafayette faced the distrust of King Louis XVI and his own family. However, when the king heard of his great popularity because of Lafayette's American adventures, the king welcomed him to the palace. This gave Lafayette the opportunity to raise money and support for the American Revolution and resulted in France sending troops and supplies to aid the Americans.

Lafayette sailed back to America in March 1780. The help Lafayette brought from France marked a turning point in the Revolutionary War. The American and French forces together were able to force General Charles Cornwallis to surrender on October 19, 1781, bringing an end to the Revolution.

After the war Lafayette returned to France. He played a role in the French

Revolution, at one point saving the royal family from a Paris mob in October 1789. He did much to strengthen the ties between France and the new nation of the United States through his friendships with Washington and **Thomas Jefferson**.

Congress granted him land in Louisiana in 1804 and eventually voted to pay him $200,000 for his Revolutionary War services.

Lafayette died in Paris on May 20, 1834. His grave is in Picpus Cemetery there.

JAMES MONROE

THE PROTECTION POLICY PRESIDENT
1758–1831

My plan of life is now fixed.

—James Monroe

President James Monroe carefully planned his words for his annual address to Congress. It had been almost twenty years since he and Robert Livingston had negotiated the purchase of the Louisiana Territory from France in 1803. Now Russia was claiming its border reached to the Oregon Territory. European powers were planning to start settlements in South America. Monroe wanted the world to know the United States would not tolerate interference from those outside the Western Hemisphere. When he addressed Congress on December 22, 1823, he firmly declared: "The American continents, by the free and independent condition which they have assumed and maintain, are henceforth not to be considered as subjects for future colonization by any European powers."

James Monroe was born in Westmoreland County, Virginia, on April 28, 1758. He was one of five children born to Spence and Elizabeth Jones Monroe. As a schoolboy and until he was sixteen, James walked several miles to Parson Campbell's school each day. "Tall, raw-boned, solemn, plain looking" was how a friend described Monroe when he enrolled at the College of William and Mary. A year later he left college and enlisted in the Third Virginia Regiment of the Continental army.

Monroe was seriously wounded at the Battle of Trenton in New Jersey in December 1776. He survived the winter of 1778–1779 with General **George Washington** at Valley Forge, Pennsylvania, and fought in the Battle of Monmouth, also in New Jersey.

After the war Monroe returned to Virginia and studied law under Governor **Thomas Jefferson**. This experience proved to be the turning point of his life. With Jefferson's help, he was elected as a Virginia delegate to the Congress of Confederation, the governing body of the United States after it won independence from Britain and prior to the adoption of the **Constitution of the United States of America** in 1789.

Monroe traveled throughout what was known as the Northwest Territories (the Great Lakes and Ohio River region) in 1784. The experience gave him the firsthand knowledge he needed to help form the laws that established territorial governments for the western lands.

In 1786 Monroe married Elizabeth Kortright. She was a very beautiful woman from New York City. Like Monroe, she was often solemn and formal.

They had two daughters, as well as a son who died in infancy.

Monroe could not stay away from politics. He opened a law practice in Fredericksburg, Virginia, and returned as a delegate to the Virginia convention called to ratify (accept) the Constitution. He voted against it! He was a veteran of the Revolutionary War who still carried scars from the wounds he received fighting for America's independence. He feared the Constitution would give the government too much power.

By the time he was elected senator from Virginia in 1790, Monroe had became a strong supporter of the Constitution. He served as senator for three years before becoming the U.S. representative to France.

From 1799 to 1803, Monroe was governor of Virginia. President Jefferson, confident of Monroe's abilities, sent him to France in 1803 to help negotiate the Louisiana Purchase. Working with the diplomat Robert Livingston, Monroe helped add more than 800,000 square miles to the United States. The territory added included present-day Arkansas, Missouri, Iowa, North Dakota, South Dakota, Nebraska, and Oklahoma; most of Kansas; parts of Montana, Wyoming, Colorado, and Minnesota, and, of course, Louisiana!

Monroe then became minister to Britain. He hoped to stop the British from harassing American ships and kidnapping American sailors through diplomacy. That mission failed. The United States declared war on Britain in 1812. Monroe served as secretary of state under President **James Madison** and led the Maryland militia (citizen soldiers) in an unsuccessful attempt to keep Washington, D.C. from being invaded.

In 1816 James Monroe was elected the fifth president of the United States. It was a time some called the "era of good feeling," because there were few political battles, and the nation was not at war. Along with his efforts to build roads and canals and improve trade within the states, Monroe pressed for policies to protect the nation, urging Congress to "build up America's armed forces" to prevent invasions and attacks.

"Our land and naval forces should be adequate to do the necessary," he said. This was not a popular policy. People wanted to move away from war, and the nation was in a financial crisis. Nevertheless, Monroe and his brilliant secretary of state, **John Quincy Adams**, led the United States to assume Spain's debt of five million dollars to American citizens in exchange for ownership of Florida. Monroe believed this territory would be essential in maintaining the nation's security.

In 1820 Monroe signed the Missouri Compromise, which allowed Missouri to enter the union as a slave state; Maine and all the other territories of the Louisiana Purchase that joined the union would be slave-free states. Monroe was a slaveholder who feared the issue of slavery would divide the nation. In 1816 he helped found the American Colonization Society to help African Americans who were not slaves return to Africa and establish a settlement where they would have full citizenship. This did nothing, however, to help those who were still slaves in America.

Monroe was able to persuade Congress to provide finances for the American Colonization Society's efforts. Over the next decade the society relocated 2,638 African Americans to the colony that became the independent African state of Liberia in 1842. Its capital, Monrovia, is named in his honor.

In 1825 a woman attending a farewell reception at the White House for President Monroe described him as "tall . . . his dress plain . . . his manner quiet and dignified." He had changed little from the sixteen-year-old boy who left Parson Campbell's school and enrolled in college. His steadfast integrity and dedication to his country had not wavered from his days as a soldier fighting in the Revolutionary War. The man he had most admired, Thomas Jefferson, said, "Monroe was so honest that if you turned his soul inside out there would not be a spot on it."

Monroe died on July 4, 1831, and is buried in Richmond, Virginia. It would be another twenty years before the words he spoke, declaring the Western Hemisphere "off limits" to European colonization, became known around the world as the Monroe Doctrine.

DEBORAH SAMSON GANNETT
(AKA ROBERT SHURTLEFF)

SOLDIER IN DISGUISE
1760–1827

*T*he whole history of the American Revolution furnishes no other similar example of female heroism to compare with Deborah Samson.

—The Committee on Revolutionary Pensions, 1837

Unhappy with traditional roles of women in wartime and angry with the British, Deborah Samson made a shocking decision. She disguised herself as a man and enlisted in the Continental army in 1782. She fought as a soldier for seventeen months without anyone else knowing she was a woman, until a musket-ball wound ended her career.

Samson was born on December 17, 1760, in Plympton, Massachusetts. Her father left to go to sea when she was five. Reports listed him as lost. In fact, he had abandoned his family and moved to Maine. While still a young girl, Deborah went to work for Deacon Jeremiah Thomas as an indentured servant helping to care for his ten sons. Indentured servants agreed to work for someone for a certain period of time in exchange for food and shelter and a life that was little better than slavery.

Farm girls did not attend the few public schools that existed during this time. They usually learned to read and write by cross-stitching letters and numbers on pieces of cloth called samplers. Deborah persuaded the Thomas boys to review their schoolwork with her each night to advance her reading and writing skills.

When she was eighteen, Samson began work as a schoolteacher in Middlesboro, Massachusetts. She made extra money by spinning and weaving at Sproat's Tavern, where she listened to stories of the Revolutionary War. Taverns during this time were meeting places where people ate, drank, and rested. Samson's thirst for adventure and love for her country grew, but she wanted to do more than carry pitchers of water or make bandages, which were the usual duties of women who went to work in the soldiers' camps near the battlefields. She wanted to fight for her country as a soldier. "I knew I would have to pretend to be a man to do so," she later told audiences who paid to hear her describe her wartime experiences.

Samson cut her hair, dressed in men's clothing, and walked to Bellingham, Massachusetts, where she enlisted in the Fourth Regiment of the Continental army. According to documents in the National Archives, where the government keeps its historical records, she signed up on May 20, 1782, as Robert Shurtleff.

Some other records show the spelling as *Shurtliff*. At five feet, eight inches, she was taller than many men. She had large facial features and concealed her figure by binding her chest with rags. Three days later she and forty-nine men joined Captain George Webb's company.

Years of hard labor on the Thomas farm had made Samson physically strong. Fellow soldiers often talked about Shurtleff's strength and stamina. They admired Shurtleff's courage, fighting skills, and loyalty. She slept in her clothing and bathed at night, when everyone else was asleep. The other soldiers never knew Shurtleff was a woman in disguise!

The British continued to occupy New York City after the British general Charles Cornwallis surrendered at Yorktown, New York, in 1781. In October 1782, they ambushed the Continental army near Tarrytown, New York. In that hand-to-hand skirmish, a saber cut Samson's forehead, and a musket ball pierced her thigh.

Samson permitted the doctor to treat her head wound but hid her thigh wound and used her knife to dig the musket ball from her leg. An infection the doctors called brain fever developed. As the fever worsened, Samson fell unconscious. The doctor treating Samson for the fever discovered she was a woman and took her to his home to recover. When she could travel, he notified her commanding officer of her true identity. She was quietly and honorably discharged from the army. Neither the doctor nor her commanding officer revealed her secret to anyone else.

Samson returned home and married Benjamin Gannett. She petitioned the Massachusetts General Court for funds available to those who had served as soldiers. **Paul Revere** investigated her claim and recommended it be granted. When the legislature awarded Samson a small sum of money in recognition of her service to the patriots, Governor **John Hancock** signed the document.

Revere also talked with President **George Washington** about Samson's service. Washington invited her to the capital and granted her land and a pension (income) of four dollars a month in gratitude for her service. She became the first woman granted a federal pension. The funds were not enough to meet her needs, however, so she began traveling the country, wearing her old uniform and giving rousing patriotic talks about the war. Advertisements hailed her as "The American Heroine."

Deborah Samson died in her son's home in Sharon, Massachusetts, on April 19, 1827. She is buried in Rock Ridge Cemetery. On May 23, 1983, Governor Michael J. Dukakis signed a proclamation naming Samson the Official Heroine of the Commonwealth of Massachusetts. In 1985 the United States Capitol Historical Society issued a commemorative medal in her honor. She became the first American woman to serve in uniform as a soldier, and the first official heroine of any state.

SYBIL LUDINGTON

HEROINE WHO RODE FOR FREEDOM
1761–1839

 *will.*

—Sybil Ludington, April 26, 1777

Sybil Ludington tucked the quilt around her sleeping younger sisters. The night of April 26, 1777, was filled with loud claps of thunder. Suddenly, above the noise of the storm, came the pounding of someone's fists on the front door.

"The British have taken Danbury," a messenger gasped as he stumbled into the house. "Two thousand British soldiers have taken all the food, horses, rifles, gunpowder and bullets, and have set the town on fire. You must gather help immediately, or we will all be ablaze."

Sybil was born on April 5, 1761, in Fredericksburg, New York. She was the oldest of twelve children born to Henry and Abigail Ludington. As the messenger told of the burning of Danbury, Connecticut, Colonel Ludington tried to hide his concern, but he did not fool Sybil. She knew the men her father commanded in the New York militia (citizen soldiers) were scattered throughout the countryside, planting their spring crops. The Revolutionary War had been under way for less than a year, and already it had taken a terrible toll on the men struggling to care for their families while staying prepared to fight. Sybil had secretly wished she could do more for the patriot cause and to help her father. Tonight might be her chance!

Colonel Ludington struggled with the dilemma. He could not ride through the night to gather his men and at the same time organize the militia. And the exhausted messenger certainly could ride no further. "Who will sound the alarm?" he asked his wife. "I will," Sybil quickly volunteered.

Her father protested for only a moment. He had no choice. He also had confidence in the daughter he had taught to ride at an early age. She had often traveled with him on his militia duties. If anyone could cover forty miles on horseback in the storm, avoid the British soldiers, and escape any outlaws on the route, Sybil could.

Like many other girls of colonial times, Sybil had been taught that wearing men's clothing was a sin. She told her mother she would not disgrace herself by wearing trousers even for the cause of patriotism. Instead, she gathered her ankle-length skirt over a pair of leggings, which would allow her to ride using a man's saddle without difficulty.

Sybil may not have even taken time to saddle her bay horse, Star. After wrapping her heavy woolen cape around her shoulders, she mounted Star, grabbed a stick with one hand and the reins with the other, and headed into the dangerous night.

For forty miles she rode, south through Carmel and Mahopac, north past Red Mills and Redding Corners, then finally through Pecksville into Stormville. At each home along the route, she banged her stick against the shutters until someone came to the window or the door. "The British are burning Danbury! Gather your goods and muster at Ludington's!"

Her voice hoarse and her clothing soaked, Sybil slipped by the camps of sleeping British soldiers. Star's black mane, tail, and legs made her a difficult target to spot in the darkness, while the red glow of Danbury burning cast eerie shadows across the cloudy sky.

I must keep riding! I must keep riding! The words beat in Sybil's head in rhythm with Star's steady hoof beats. She thought of how fortunate she was to have a father who had taught her to be such a fearless rider.

Cheering soldiers greeted Sybil as she and Star arrived back home near dawn. Her father's company of soldiers had gathered and marched on Danbury, driving the British soldiers back to their ships in Long Island Sound. The patriots claimed victory at what became known as the Battle of Ridgefield.

In 1784 Sybil married a New York attorney, Edmond Ogden. Ogden served with **John Paul Jones** during the Revolutionary War. The Ogdens had one son.

Sybil Ludington Ogden died on February 26, 1839. She is buried near her father in the Maple Avenue Cemetery in Putnam County, New York. The headstone spells her name "Sibbell." Another spelling of her name, *Sebel*, appears in her husband's military records.

Unlike many other young women who risked their lives during the Revolutionary War, Sybil Ludington has not been forgotten. A statue on Route 52 in Carmel, New York, shows Sybil on her horse with a stick in her hand, ready to ride to summon her father's troops. A smaller copy of the statue is displayed in Constitution Memorial Hall in the Washington, D.C., headquarters of the Daughters of the American Revolution.

In 1976, as part of the nation's bicentennial celebration, the U.S. Postal Service issued a commemorative stamp honoring "youthful heroine" Sybil Ludington riding Star. In 1995 the National Rifle Association established the Sybil Ludington Women's Freedom Award "to honor women with courage, spirit, daring, and perseverance."

Each year on the weekend nearest April 26, the Taconic Road Runners Club of New York holds the Sybil Ludington Fifty-Kilometer Historical Run. The runners start and finish in Carmel, passing through several of the towns through which Ludington rode. No horses are allowed, however, and none of the runners wear ankle-length skirts and woolen capes.

EMILY GEIGER

It is trusted her name will descend to posterity.

—From *Beauties of the Revolution*, published in 1859

Different versions of events written at different times by different writers often result in historical stories that are part truth and part fiction. The story of Emily Geiger is one of these. Hundreds of books, plays, and documentaries have presented the story of Geiger's daring service as an American patriot. Her story appears in collections of folklore and on pages of textbooks as fact. Historians challenge, scholars argue, and family researchers defend her actual existence. All agree that she is one of the most well known unknowns of the American Revolution.

What *is* known is that the Continental army General **Nathanael Greene** was in a tough spot during the southern campaign in South Carolina in June 1781. He and his weary troops had retreated from a location known as Ninety-Six. The British, led by Lord Rawdon, were following in hot pursuit. Greene believed that if he could get word to General Thomas Sumter one hundred miles away, their two patriot armies could combine and retake Ninety-Six.

Greene needed a courier to carry to Sumter word of Greene's plan. With no satellites, computers, telephones, or telegraphs available at that time, Greene had to ask for volunteers from his men to carry the message. No one volunteered. Each man knew there would be British soldiers and sympathizers along the route. If he were caught, he would have no one to help him fight, and he would be hung.

What follows is John A. Chapman's version of the Geiger legend, published in *School History of South Carolina* in 1897. Emily Geiger's father was committed to the American fight for independence, but he was an invalid. When she overheard a friend telling him about Greene's request, she went to see Greene and volunteered for the mission. Greene hesitated. This young woman would be traveling alone on horseback, and it would take her three days to reach Sumter. Geiger insisted, and Greene finally agreed. He wrote his message and gave it to her, but he required her to memorize every word he had written in case she was captured. When she could repeat the message without reading it, General Greene gave her a horse (some versions say the horse's name was Black Dan), and she headed for Sumter's camp.

Living near the Geiger's home was a man named Lowry who was loyal to the British. About four hours after Geiger left to carry the message, Lowry learned of her mission and sent a man to follow her. That evening, he stopped at the home of Billy Mink, another of Lowry's spies. Mink decided to take his best horse and chase her himself. He assumed she would stop at a nearby settlement, where it would be safe for her to spend the night.

Geiger had other ideas. She circled the settlement and rode away to a house owned by the Preston family, who were friends of her family. She asked if she could spend the night. The Prestons were on the side of the British. They gave Geiger a place to rest, not knowing the true reason for her travels.

About two hours after Geiger went to sleep, galloping hoof beats awakened her. She listened from behind the door of the bedroom to Billy Mink ask Mrs. Preston of her whereabouts. He told Mrs. Preston that Geiger must be stopped from reaching General Sumter.

"Why don't you rest for the night, and in the morning when she awakes you may question her," Mrs. Preston suggested. She did not deny Geiger was there, but she did not want Geiger to be harmed even if she was helping the patriots.

Geiger waited until she knew Mink was asleep. Then she slipped out the window and rode on to the Elwood home a few miles away. The Elwoods were supporters of the Americans. When Geiger told them of her mission, they gave her a fresh horse and a letter addressed to a friend twenty miles away, instructing him to give Geiger a fresh horse when she arrived.

By the end of the second day, Geiger had covered almost two-thirds of the distance. Her luck ran out when three British soldiers stopped her. Geiger lied about her destination, but the soldiers did not believe her answers and took her to Lord Rawdon for questioning. Lord Rawdon did not believe her answers, either. He sent for a Tory (British supporter) woman to come and search her for messages.

The soldiers took Geiger to an upstairs bedroom in a nearby home to wait. As soon as they left her alone, she frantically tore the message into tiny pieces. But where could she hide the pieces?

Bit by bit, she began swallowing the torn paper. When the woman arrived to search her, Geiger's mouth was still full of the bits of paper. She flung herself face down across the bed and pretended to be sobbing to give herself enough time to swallow all traces of the message.

After searching Geiger, the woman reported that she could find no messages. An embarrassed Lord Rawdon apologized to Geiger and told her she could leave, even providing her with an escort to take her to the friends she named, who lived six miles away.

When it was safe, Geiger rode on all night with a guide who knew a short-cut to Sumter's camp. When daylight came, the guide turned back. Geiger kept riding alone.

About three o'clock that afternoon, Emily Geiger saw patriot soldiers and told them of her mission. They took her to General Sumter, where she delivered Greene's dispatch from memory. Within an hour General Sumter and his troops were on their way to meet Greene. Four months later the Revolutionary War ended with victory for the American patriots.

Chapman based his story on a book by Mrs. Elizabeth F. Ellet titled *Women of the American Revolution*, published in 1848. More stories about Geiger began appearing about the time of the nation's 150th birthday in 1926. Women's magazines and southern family histories described in great detail Geiger's marriage to a man named John Threrwitts on October 18, 1789, and told about a set of jeweled brooches and earrings given to Emily by General Greene on the morning of her wedding. Of course this was impossible, because Greene had died three years earlier, in 1786. Other versions claim to know the secret location of Geiger's grave.

Whatever version is true, there can be no doubt that the story of Emily Geiger represents the spirit of the brave women who helped America win independence.

JOHN QUINCY ADAMS

THE PRESIDENT WHO WOULD NOT QUIT
1767–1848

You will never know how much it has cost my generation to preserve your freedom.

—John Quincy Adams

He had achieved the goal of his lifetime, but John Quincy Adams was not happy. The sixth president of the United States of America believed he had never succeeded at anything except becoming unpopular. He had gone home to Massachusetts after being defeated for a second term as president when a knock on his door late one evening turned Adams's sadness to joy: His neighbors wanted him to run for Congress!

John Quincy Adams was born July 11, 1767, in Braintree (now Quincy), Massachusetts. His parents were **John Adams** and Abigail Smith Adams. Both were active supporters of the growing opposition to British rule in the colonies. John Adams would later become the second president of the United States. They devoted themselves to providing their children with the best education possible. Latin, mathematics, and reading were part of oldest son John Quincy's daily lessons.

A lesson John Quincy learned when he was nearly eight years old stayed with him for the rest of his life. On June 17, 1775, he watched from his home as the ill-prepared Continental army fought the well-trained British soldiers at Bunker Hill. The sights, sounds, and smells of the battle impressed him so deeply that he promised himself he would devote himself to serving his country.

The following year John Quincy learned that his father had signed the **Declaration of Independence**. Young Adams worried that the British would take his family prisoner and hang his father as a traitor for signing the document that officially announced that the United States would no longer be ruled by the British.

Instead of being captured and hung, his father was sent to Europe to help win friends for the American Revolution. He took his sons, John Quincy and Charles Francis, with him. For the next six years they worked as aides to their father and studied fencing, dance, music, art, and languages. John Quincy enrolled at Leiden University in Amsterdam. By the time he was fourteen, he could write and speak so many languages so well that the American minister to Russia hired him as his personal secretary.

In 1785 John Quincy returned to the United States and enrolled in Harvard College. He then became a lawyer, but spent most of his time arguing politics instead of cases for his clients. Shortly after his father became vice president of the United States, John Quincy was appointed as President **George Washington**'s representative to the Netherlands. He later became a diplomat (government representative) in London, where he married Louisa Catherine Johnson on July 26, 1797.

Adams was elected to the U.S. Senate in 1803. Six years later, however, the people of Massachusetts replaced him with another senator because of his support of actions by the federal government that they did not like, including the Louisiana Purchase. This was the beginning of Adams's unhappiness with politics, though he desperately wanted to serve his country. President **James Madison** made him ambassador to Russia; he negotiated the treaty that ended the War of 1812; he served as ambassador to England; and he became secretary of state to President **James Monroe** from 1817 to 1825. Adams did so much during these years to help establish policies and treaties for the United States that he was certain he could win the vote to become the sixth president in 1825.

He did, but not without accusations that he acted improperly to gain the support of another candidate, Henry Clay. During the next four years, the moody President Adams ignored his critics and pushed on with his programs. He especially wanted Congress to finance scientific expeditions and experiments. Unfortunately, he became known more for his quick temper when Congress disagreed with him than for his leadership.

Each morning Adams arose early, made his own fire, then took a walk or swam in the Potomac River. Louisa spent most of her time alone, writing. She actively worked to help Adams get reelected. He believed he should be elected just because of the things he had already done for the country. When he was defeated for a second term as president, he wrote in his diary that his whole life had been "a series of disappointments." This included his family life. Two of their four children had died tragic deaths. John Quincy and Louisa returned to Massachusetts, where he expected to die a forgotten failure.

Adams was a bitter, sick man when his neighbors asked him to do something no other president had done before: They wanted him to return to Congress as their representative. Inspired by their confidence and eager to be heard by those who had not listened to him before, Adams agreed. He easily won election and returned to Washington, ready to do battle. The southern states had passed a "gag rule" prohibiting any petitions or mentions of legislation to abolish (do away with) the practice of slavery. Adams took on the entire U.S. Congress by refusing to be "gagged." He accused Congress of violating the **Constitution of the United States of America**. A constitution is a set of rules and laws that tells how a government is organized and run.

Day after day Adams would introduce petitions from citizens seeking to abolish slavery. Each time he spoke, he was ordered to be quiet. He would start on a new subject, but would insert antislavery petitions as he talked. Though Adams was much older than most of the other representatives, his enthusiasm kept him arguing long after others had given up. He stood alone and he stood often, even when he received death threats, and attempts were made to have him arrested by those who did not want to see the slavery issue debated. Adams earned the titles "Mad Old Man from Massachusetts" and "Old Man Eloquent."

In December 1844 Adams called for another vote to remove the gag rule. The motion passed, and opposition to slavery could no longer be kept silent in Congress.

John Quincy Adams died of a stroke on February 23, 1848. He was eighty. For eighteen years he had served in the House of Representatives after his term as president of the United States. He is buried with his parents in the Adams family tomb in Quincy, Massachusetts.

ANDREW JACKSON

HERO OF NEW ORLEANS
1767–1845

He's tough—tough as old hickory.

—A soldier in General Andrew Jackson's army

The British officer glared at his lanky captive. It was not unusual for American boys this young to volunteer as messengers in 1780 for the militia (citizen soldiers). This boy with fiery red hair and his older brother had been captured near Camden, South Carolina. What fools they were, the officer told them, to join with other rebel colonists in the War of Independence. "I order you to kneel and polish my boots," commanded the officer. Thirteen-year-old Andrew Jackson refused.

The officer drew his sword and slashed Jackson's hand and head. Someday, Jackson vowed to his brother as they were shoved into prison, *he* would hold the sword and would make the British kneel.

Andrew Jackson's parents and his two older brothers, Hugh and Robert, came to America from Ireland. His father died just a few weeks before Andrew's birth on March 15, 1767. His mother moved the family west, and Andrew learned to read in a frontier school. He would often read newspapers aloud to his neighbors who could not read.

Growing up on the frontier enabled Andrew and his brothers to become expert riders and marksmen (shooters). Their daring skirmishes with Loyalists (British supporters) led to an encounter in which Hugh, Andrew's oldest brother, was killed.

While Andrew and Robert were in prison after being captured at Camden, an epidemic of smallpox broke out, and Robert died. Andrew's mother volunteered to nurse the American prisoners in Charleston, South Carolina, later that year. By doing so she won freedom for Andrew, but she caught cholera and died.

After the war Andrew tried his hand at saddle making and teaching school to earn a living. At age eighteen he decided to study law. It was customary at that time for someone who wanted to be a lawyer to study under a practicing lawyer rather than attend law school. Jackson stood over six feet tall, and his commanding presence in the courtroom helped him win many cases. He also bought and sold land and became a wealthy bachelor. Jackson fell in love with Rachel Robards, who was separated from her husband. Jackson and Rachel believed that her husband had obtained a divorce, and they were married in 1791. Unfortunately, Rachel's first husband had not obtained a divorce, and this led to problems for Jackson several years later.

When the State of Tennessee was formed in 1796, Jackson wasted no time making a name for himself as its elected representative. A year later he was elected senator and served until 1798. He then served on the state supreme court.

At that time the enormous British fleet needed sailors to work on its ships. It began capturing American ships and kidnapping sailors, forcing them to serve on British ships. These acts of human piracy, along with the British efforts to help the Indians stop settlers from moving west, resulted in America's declaring war on Britain in 1812. Though suffering from various illnesses, Jackson did not hesitate to join the fight. From the Hermitage, his plantation near Nashville, Tennessee, Jackson helped to raise and fund an army of volunteers. The first mission he led was not a success; the second was.

The Upper Creek Indians had joined with the British against the settlers, who were moving into their lands. When the Upper Creek raided Fort Mims in what is now Alabama and killed 250 settlers, Jackson was ordered to lead a force against them. At the Battle of Horseshoe Bend, Jackson allowed the Indian women and children to cross the Tallapoosa River to safety. He then defeated the Creek warriors with the help of **Sam Houston** and the Cherokee warrior **Sequoyah**. The Cherokee had sided with the settlers against the Creek. "He's tough—tough as old hickory," one of Jackson's men said of him. The nickname fit Jackson perfectly.

In 1814 the opportunity that "Old Hickory" had secretly longed for arrived. He was ordered to New Orleans to defend the city on the mouth of the Mississippi River against the British. He recruited almost five thousand defenders, including African Americans, Frenchmen, and members of the Tennessee and Kentucky militias. The war would be lost, Jackson told the volunteers, if the United States did not keep control of New Orleans.

The British had planned a surprise attack on New Orleans, but Jackson learned of it and had his troops ready. Although the British forces outnumbered Jackson's defenders two to one, Jackson's brilliant strategies stopped them. When the cannon smoke cleared, the man with no formal military training who had come from his sickbed to fight had defeated the most feared army in the world. The British had lost 1,971 soldiers; Jackson had lost 70. Ironically, neither Jackson nor the British knew that the war had officially ended two weeks earlier.

Jackson became not only the hero of New Orleans, but also the hero of the United States of America. For the next ten years his popularity grew; however, he lost his first attempt to become president in 1824 to **John Quincy Adams.**

The Jacksonians—supporters of Jackson—made good use of his nickname in the next campaign. They distributed hickory toothpicks and hickory canes, reminding people to vote for Old Hickory. The people elected him the seventh president of the United States in 1828, but Jackson's joy in winning the election turned to sadness when Rachel died of a heart attack just before he took office. He was elected to a second term in 1832.

Jackson was the first president of the United States born in a log cabin. Like President **George Washington**, he had not attended college. He delighted in serving his guests his favorite meal—turkey hash. Jackson never lost his "hero" status with his admirers, but his presidency was clouded by problems with banking, tariffs (taxes), and other economic issues.

It was most clouded by the government's treatment of Native Americans. In his first message to Congress, Jackson outlined his policy for Indian removal, and Congress passed the Indian Removal Act of 1830. This act did not order the removal of any Indians, but gave the president the right to negotiate treaties to exchange tribal lands in the east for lands west of the Mississippi River. Jackson and the government promised that relocations would be voluntary, but they were forced. He violated Indian treaties and land deals, always defending his actions as intended for the good of the Indians, which was not true. Some four thousand Cherokee Indians died during the 1838–1839 forced removal from their eastern lands on a thousand-mile march known as the Trail of Tears or, as a direct translation from the Cherokee language, The Trail Where They Cried.

An attempt was made on Jackson's life on January 30, 1835. The attacker fired pistols at Jackson in the Capitol, missing both times. The aging president responded by beating the attacker with his cane.

After his presidency Jackson returned to the Hermitage, where he died of tuberculosis (a bacterial disease) in 1845. His pet parrot, Poll, was among the mourners at his burial.

In his will Andrew Jackson left his nephew "the elegant sword presented to me by the state of Tennessee." It was the sword he had worn when the British surrendered at New Orleans.

DOLLEY MADISON

PATRIOT OF THE PEOPLE'S HOUSE
1768–1849

Our private property must be sacrificed.

—Dolley Madison

First Lady Dolley Payne Todd Madison did not know how to dance, paint, or speak foreign languages. None of those things mattered on August 23, 1814, when she hastily filled her trunk with important government documents and escaped just hours before the invading British army set fire to the people's house in Washington, D.C.

Dolley was born on May 20, 1768, in Guilford County, North Carolina. She was one of eight children born to Mary Coles Payne and John Payne. Her father was a slaveholder in North Carolina, but when he married Mary Coles, he became a Quaker. As a Quaker he was not allowed to own slaves, so in 1783 he sold his plantation, freed his slaves, and moved to Philadelphia. He opened a business as a starch merchant.

In 1790 Dolley married John Todd, a lawyer. They had two children, John and William. Dolley's husband and their son, William, died of yellow fever (a disease spread by mosquitoes) in 1793.

Less than one year later the twenty-six-year-old widow met **James Madison**, a forty-three-year-old bachelor. Madison was already a well-known politician. He had been an important contributor to the writing and ratification (acceptance) of the **Constitution of the United States of America**. A constitution is a set of rules and laws that tells how a government is organized and run.

James was a quiet, shy, brilliant man. Dolley was a tall, dark-haired beauty whose warmth and outgoing charm captured his heart. Up until this time she had always dressed simply in dark colors. Her attraction to Madison caused a change in her wardrobe to fancier dresses, and she began wearing powder and rouge. "The great little Madison . . . has asked to see me this evening," Dolley wrote to a girlfriend. The courtship of Dolley and James became the talk of Philadelphia.

Dolley and "Jemmy" were married in September 1794, while he was serving in the U.S. House of Representatives. In 1797 he left politics and moved his new family to Montpelier, his home in Virginia. He intended to live quietly as a farmer, but President **Thomas Jefferson** asked him to serve as his secretary of state. The Madisons moved to Washington, D.C., in 1801.

When the Madisons arrived, Washington was a small, new settlement still under construction. The population of the city was about three thousand people. It had been chosen as the capital of the new U.S. government in 1790. **John**

Adams had been the first president to live in the unfinished mansion then known as the President's Palace. Dolley took over the job as hostess for President Jefferson. She became the most popular woman in Washington, though she said that she conducted her social activities as a patriotic duty, not for popularity.

Dolley's social influence contributed greatly to her husband's becoming president in 1809. The Madisons moved into an empty house because the previous presidents who had lived there had provided their own furnishings. Dolley believed the furnishings should belong to the nation, so with a budget provided by Congress and working with architect Benjamin Latrobe, she made the home of the president "the people's house" with "public spaces." She made sure the furnishings were elegant, but not like those of the castles of Europe, to represent the look of a new and independent nation. The wedding in 1812 of her sister, Lucy, was the first wedding held there.

Just thirty years after America won independence from Britain, the British navy began attacking American ships and taking sailors as well as cargo. The United States declared war against Britian in 1812. On the morning of August 24, 1814, a soldier who had gone with President Madison to review the troops outside of Washington came riding back to the president's house, ordering, "Clear out! Clear out!" The British were invading and burning Washington, D.C.!

According to a letter Dolley wrote to her sister, she gathered some of the dining-room silver, packed her trunk with important papers from Madison's office, and sent the silver and trunk by wagon to the Bank of Maryland.

She steadfastly remained at the house until she saw some of the British soldiers approaching the front gates. She was determined to save the portrait of General **George Washington** painted by the artist Gilbert Stuart. Since there was no time to unscrew the frame, she ordered that the frame be broken and the "precious painting" removed and carried to safety "in the hands of two gentlemen of New York." The painting went one direction, and Dolley went in another in her small buggy with one of her servants. She took with her none of the Madisons' personal belongings. When the British arrived, they ate the food that had been prepared for the Madisons' lunch and then set fire to the inside of the house.

The Americans defeated the British in the War of 1812 (1812–1815), but the Madisons never lived in the house again. They lived in another building in Washington while arguments raged about moving the capital to another location. Repairs to the house were finally begun, and President **James Monroe** moved into it in 1817. The painting of George Washington that Dolley saved was returned and hangs today in the White House, as the home of the president has been called since 1901.

At the end of President Madison's second term, the couple retired permanently to Montpelier. After her husband's death in 1836, Dolley moved back to Washington. She and James had no children together, but she was forced to sell Montpelier to pay off the debts generated by her son from her first marriage. She spent her last days in near poverty. A few months before her death, Congress agreed to purchase her collection of James Madison's papers for $25,000.

Dolley died on July 12, 1849. Washington newspapers reported, "Citizens and strangers lined the streets as the funeral procession went by to honor the patriot of the people's house." She is buried beside James at the family cemetery at Montpelier.

AFRICAN AMERICAN PATRIOTS

FIRST TO FIGHT FOR AMERICA'S FREEDOM
1770–1850

Those whom liberty has cost nothing do not know how to prize it.

—Dr. Harris, African American
Revolutionary War veteran, 1842

"Prince Jenks . . . Samson Hazzard . . .
Scipio Brown . . . Philo Phillips . . ."
The Honorable Tristam Burges stood
before the Congress of Rhode Island
on a cold day in January 1828 and
slowly read the names of the men of
the First Rhode Island Regiment:

Crispus Attucks

"Thomas Brown . . . Cato Greene . . . York Champlin . . . Primus Rhodes . . ."

Fifty years earlier these men had responded to a call from the Rhode Island General Assembly for "every able-bodied Negro, Mulatto, and Indian slave" to enlist to fight the British. Any men who enlisted would receive the same wages as free men; slave recruits who served three years were to be given a certificate of manumission (release from slavery).

Slavery had been legally recognized in America since 1650, in part because of the growing need for laborers and also because many of the people coming to America had lived in countries where slavery was practiced. According to the Rhode Island Black Heritage Society, "Although slave trade and plantations were considered to be a southern way of life in 1778, they also existed outside the South. A number of Rhode Island slaves gained their freedom enlisting in the first black army unit in the American Revolutionary War."

An estimated five thousand people of African American heritage served in the American army and navy during the Revolutionary War. At first General **George Washington** forbade the enlistment of slaves or ex-slaves in the Continental army. Washington knew that colonists feared arming slaves, and he thought they would not be needed. By 1778, however, the need for more soldiers was so severe that Washington changed his mind and suggested that Rhode Island recruit slaves with an offer that would include freedom if they served their time satisfactorily.

Another factor in Washington's decision was the news that the royal governor of Virginia, John Murray, had promised to free all slaves who would join "the king's army." Murray threatened to have "all the slaves in America on the side of the [British] government." A large number of slaves did join with the British, but many did not trust the British and feared they would become slaves of the British once the war was over.

Many slaves were also inspired by the story of the African American Crispus Attucks, called "the first to die for independence" after he was killed on March 5,

1770, at what became known as the Boston Massacre. Attucks and a group of other Boston colonists were harassing British soldiers who had been sent to America to discourage the colonists from rebelling. When Attucks and others rushed toward the soldiers ordering them to leave the area, he was shot twice in the chest by the soldiers, who also killed four of his patriot friends.

The names of many African American freedom fighters are unknown; those of others, such as Quack Matrick and Prince Richards, are known because records show they drew a pension (government payment) after the war was over. Pensions for soldiers who could prove they had faithfully served the patriot cause averaged around eight dollars a month. Not all slaves who were promised their freedom for serving received what they had been promised, however. Those who did were identified as "free people of color" but were still denied full rights as citizens of the United States.

The importation of slaves was banned in America in 1808, but the law did not stop illegal slave trafficking. The British began capturing American ships, taking the cargo and forcing the crews to serve on British ships. President **James Madison** led the United States to declare war on Britain in 1812, and African Americans were invited to serve as seamen and soldiers for the United States. Slaves were again offered their freedom for doing so, and again many were denied what they had fought for, including those who volunteered to fight in the Battle of New Orleans under General **Andrew Jackson**.

During both the Revolutionary War and the War of 1812 (1812–1815), African Americans served as spies, sounded the commands on the battlefields as **drummers and fifers**, fought as minutemen, and provided the crews needed to keep naval ships operating. If captured by the British, they became prisoners of war.

A year after Texas became a slave state in 1845, the United States declared war on Mexico over disputed land. Records of the First Regiment of Volunteers, New York; the Fourth Artillery; and the Ninth, Tenth, Eleventh, and Thirteenth

Infantry regiments include many names of African American soldiers who served as volunteers in General **Zachary Taylor**'s army. Taylor, a slaveholder, became the twelfth president of the United States in 1849. He refused to side with slaveholding states who wanted to secede (withdraw) from the United States while he was president.

African Americans served the cause of liberty, though most were denied the rights and privileges they had helped secure. Later events that brought an end to these injustices were made possible by their extraordinary patriotic contributions.

SEQUOYAH

(AKA GEORGE GIST OR GUESS)

CHEROKEE WARRIOR
C. 1770–1843

He who fights my enemies is my friend.

—Words attributed to Sequoyah sewn on
a nineteenth-century cross-stitch sampler

On the morning of March 27, 1814, General **Andrew Jackson** arrived at Horseshoe Bend on the Tallapoosa River near what is today Daviston, Alabama. Among the 3,300 men who arrived with him was a part-Cherokee warrior who walked with a severe limp.

Sequoyah (Sikwo-yi) was born in about 1770 to Wu-te-he, the daughter of a Tsalagi (Cherokee) Indian chief, and her husband, Nathaniel Gist. (Some records give Sequoyah's father's name as *Guess*.) Historians do not agree on the cause of Sequoyah's limp. *The Cherokee Advocate* newspaper on June 26, 1845, said, "He was the victim of hydro arthritic trouble in the knee joint." Because *Sikwo-yi* in Cherokee means "pig's foot," some think he was born with the disability. Other accounts state that his lameness resulted from a hunting accident when he was a young man. Whatever the cause, Sequoyah's physical handicap did not prevent him from leading an active life.

Sequoyah moved from Tennessee to Georgia as a young man. He learned the skill of silversmithing, making household items such as pots, pans, and dishes as well as jewelry and art. In 1809 a customer who bought one of Sequoyah's works recommended he sign his work the way white artists did. A farmer, Charles Hicks, showed Sequoyah how to spell his name. As Sequoyah puzzled over his name written on a piece of paper, his mind began its journey toward creating a system of writing for the Cherokee.

Sequoyah joined the U.S. Army as part of the Alabama militia (citizen soldiers). He agreed to help put an end to the troublesome attacks of the Upper Creek Indians.

On August 30, 1813, Upper Creek Indians attacked Fort Mims, Alabama, near Mobile, hoping to stop the flow of settlers who were moving into their homelands. The British, who were at war with the United States, encouraged the Upper Creek to keep fighting rather than accept the invading settlers peacefully. The British hoped that dividing the defenses of the United States might allow them to recapture the territory they had lost in the Revolutionary War.

On March 27, 1814, General Jackson led his militia forces, which included five hundred Cherokee volunteers, to Horseshoe Bend, where the Upper Creek were camped. Having fought with Jackson before, Sequoyah expected the fighting to be furious. His expectations were fully met: By sunset the Upper Creek were dead or scattered in defeat, unable to stop the onslaught of settlers.

In the thick of battle at Horseshoe Bend, Sequoyah watched as messages scribbled on bark or leaves were carried between Jackson and his commanders. As Sequoyah swam the Tallapoosa River to attack the Upper Creek from the rear, an old dream swam in his mind: *If only the Cherokee knew how to make leaves talk!*

Word spread among Sequoyah's friends and neighbors about his desire to invent a written language for his people, but his ideas were met with distrust and fear. Many saw writing as some kind of witchcraft. Even his friends thought Sequoyah was filled with demons.

By the time he married Sally Waters of the Bird Clan in 1815, Sequoyah had developed a plan for drawing a symbol for each sound spoken by the Cherokee. These eighty-six symbols made up the Cherokee alphabet. "Talking leaves" became a reality. Now the Cherokee could read and write letters, treaties, and other documents!

One of the greatest tests for Sequoyah's alphabet came in a courtroom when he read an argument about a boundary line from a sheet of paper. This convinced the Cherokee nation to adopt Sequoyah's alphabet in 1821.

Sequoyah moved his family to Cherokee lands in Arkansas to mine and sell salt. He became involved in politics and was elected in 1828 to make a trip to Washington, D.C., to negotiate favorable terms for the Arkansas Cherokee. They were being removed to Oklahoma under a treaty the Cherokee leaders had been forced to sign by President **John Quincy Adams**. Sequoyah hoped his old friend, Andrew Jackson would help him, but Jackson did not.

Sequoyah lived in Oklahoma for ten years before going to Mexico (Texas) to visit friends. He died during this visit in 1843. Before Sequoyah's death, **Sam Houston**, who had fought with him at Horseshoe Bend, had praised him for giving the Cherokee a written language. Houston said, "Your invention of the alphabet is worth more to your people than two bags full of gold in the hands of every Cherokee."

AMERICAN JEWISH PATRIOTS

SOLDIERS AND SUPPORTERS OF FREEDOM
1775–1850

Have we defeated the enemy?

—Last words of Francis Salvador

Six Jewish sailors arrived in the New World with Christopher Columbus in 1492. By the time America declared independence from Britain, there were about 2,500 Jewish colonists scattered throughout the colonies.

Mordecai Sheftall, leader of the patriots of Georgia

Like many others, they had come to America seeking fortune and freedom of worship. Though they were few in number, their contributions to winning and preserving independence were enormous.

Asser Levy served as a guard in the Continental army. One hundred and twenty years earlier, one of his ancestors had helped overturn a law in New Amsterdam (an early name for New York) that prohibited Jews from carrying weapons or serving as guards. The *Matilda*, a ship owned by Jewish merchants, brought the first **Liberty Bell** to America. David Emanuel was captured by the British at McBean's Creek in Georgia. He escaped and later became the first governor of Georgia.

Aaron Lopez, a Jewish merchant and patriot, gave his sailing ships to serve in the Revolutionary War.

Jewish guides, including Simon Nathan, Dr. Levy Meyers, and Jonas Phillips, led American soldiers through the woods and swamps near Savannah, Georgia, after the British captured the city. Mordecai Sheftall, the leader of the Georgia patriots captured at Savannah, was considered such a danger to the British that he was guarded at all times by British soldiers with their swords drawn and pointed at his throat.

Aaron Lopez came to Newport, Rhode Island, and became known as the "Merchant Prince of New England." He owned more than one hundred ships. He gave them all to the service of America during the Revolutionary War.

The highest-ranking Jewish officer in the Continental army was Colonel Solomon Bush of the Pennsylvania militia (citizen soldiers). He was severely wounded, then captured, and finally freed in a prisoner of war exchange.

Francis Salvador was born in 1747 and arrived in South Carolina from London in 1773. His grandfather had brought the first Jewish settlers to Georgia in 1733. Salvador became a leader in the frontier district known as Ninety-Six and was the first Jewish colonist elected to public office in South Carolina. He served as a delegate to the South Carolina Provincial Congress, formed to unite the colonists against British rule. The following year Salvador helped persuade other members to vote in favor of sending delegates to Philadelphia to vote for American independence as part of the Continental Congress.

On August 1, 1776, the twenty-nine-year-old Salvador became the first Jewish American killed in the Revolutionary War. As a member of the South Carolina militia, he was leading 330 men in a battle against the Cherokee Indians near his home. The Indians had been armed by the British to fight the colonists. Salvador died without knowing that America had formally declared independence.

Haym Salomon was born in Poland and came to America in 1772. He was a successful merchant in New York when he joined the Sons of Liberty, a secret organization of colonists who opposed British rule. When the Revolutionary War began, the British accused him of spying for the patriots, arrested him, and put him into prison. After his release, he again aided the colonists and was again arrested. This time the British planned to hang him, but his friends helped him escape to Philadelphia.

Salomon went to work building a new business, and in a short time he was providing food to the starving Continental army. He spoke ten languages and was able to use these skills to secure loans from several countries to help the Americans. A story is told that during Yom Kippur, the most important Jewish holy day, an urgent message came to Salomon from General **George Washington**, begging for funds. Salomon interrupted his devotions and raised the money from members of his congregation. Providing funds for Washington's army became a priority and a passion for Salomon. He used his own funds to make loans, which remained unpaid when he died in 1785.

Mordecai Noah was born in Philadelphia in 1785. His father fought in the Revolutionary War with General **Francis Marion**, the "Swamp Fox." Noah went to South Carolina to study law and began writing patriotic articles for a Charleston newspaper. His articles inspired support for America's going to war with Britain in 1812 to stop the British from capturing American ships at sea.

When the War of 1812 (1812–1815) ended, Noah moved to New York, where he published newspapers and wrote a number of patriotic plays. He used his patriotism to fight what he called "a war for truth with words" against a powerful, corrupt political organization. He then became a lawyer and served as one of the first Jewish judges in the United States. His plans to establish a Jewish colony on land near Buffalo, New York, failed. He was, however, the best-known Jewish American patriot in the United States when he died in 1851.

Other Jewish American patriots during the Revolutionary War include David Cardozo, who led the assault against the British who had captured Savannah, Georgia, and his brother, Isaac, who helped defend the harbor at Charleston.

During the War of 1812, Jewish American patriots who distinguished themselves as commanders of ships include the naval captain Levy Harby, a pirate fighter, and Uriah P. Levy, the first Jewish American to obtain the rank of commodore in the U.S. Navy.

Patriot David Camden DeLeon, the "fighting doctor" of the Mexican War of 1845, is another example of a Jewish American who served and sacrificed in this period of American history.

GEORGE GIBSON JR.

FATHER OF THE ARMY FOOD SERVICE
1775–1861

I must have rations in the most urgent way to feed my army, or all efforts to defend the southern border will cease.

—General Andrew Jackson to
General George Gibson Jr., 1818

Old Fort Gibson, built in the Oklahoma Territory in 1824, was named in honor of General George Gibson Jr., commissary general of the U.S. Army. A soldier there once estimated that if all the loaves of bread

General Gibson had provided for soldiers to eat were placed end to end, Gibson "would still be looking for someone to bake more bread."

Gibson was born at Westover Mills, Pennsylvania, on September 1, 1775. His father served in the Revolutionary War, and young George had little formal schooling. He grew up learning "letters and numbers" at home and hearing his father's stories of American soldiers fighting the British without food or other supplies.

The Continental Congress appointed General Thomas Mifflin to be the first commissary general. His job was to make contracts with suppliers for rations (food). The contractors were to deliver the food to the soldiers, but these contracts were not always honored. Many times colonists who were secretly loyal to the British would agree to provide food, but not do so. Others sold British soldiers the food instead of the American army because the Continental Congress had no money to pay for supplies. There often were no roads or wagons to transport food, and colonists were sometimes unwilling to risk taking supplies into battle areas. Soldiers who knew how to trap and hunt could provide their own food; those who did not had to trade on their own with colonists or go hungry. Many soldiers deserted the army rather than starve.

By 1795 the war was over, America had won independence, and a constitutional government was firmly in place. Gibson, now a young man on his own, went to work for a trading company in Baltimore. His math skills in the days when a pencil and a piece of paper were the only "computers" were extraordinary. He was soon promoted and placed in charge of a cargo ship trading in East India. In this job he learned to keep detailed records of the amount, location, and cost of items, such as spices, cloth, buttons, braids, ribbons, rum, and sugar.

By 1808 it appeared that the United States and Britain would go to war again. The British were capturing American ships and forcing American sailors to serve aboard the British ships. Gibson enlisted that year in the Fifth Infantry Regiment of the army. While serving as a soldier in the War of 1812 (1812–1815),

Gibson became well known for his ability to gather and transport supplies for General **Andrew Jackson**. He left the army when the war was over, thinking he would return to the trading business. Jackson and President **James Madison** had other plans: Madison asked him to be the quartermaster general of the southern division of the army. Gibson was thrilled. This meant he would serve under Jackson, now the national hero of the War of 1812 and the Battle of New Orleans. Gibson was appointed to the job on April 29, 1816. "I have sharpened my pencil for the task ahead," he said.

It was well that he did. By the time Gibson arrived in Nashville, Tennessee, the army's military supply system was in a terrible mess: Suppliers were demanding payments for supplies he did not have, and soldiers were demanding supplies for which he could not pay.

Gibson had not yet solved these problems when a new one developed. He received word that Jackson was preparing to take the Tennessee militia (citizen soldiers) on an expedition to defend the southern border, and as part of his plan he intended to cross into Spanish Florida. Gibson knew that Jackson was acting independently and that his actions would lead to war with the Seminole Indians. Nonetheless, Gibson's orders were to supply food to the soldiers, and that was what he would do. He told Jackson that he could not rely on suppliers to deliver the food because of the danger.

Before leading his troops into Florida, Jackson wisely arranged with Gibson for rations to be stored in New Orleans. The daily ration the government was to supply each soldier was one pound of salted beef or three-fourths of a pound of salted pork; one pound of bread or flour; and a half-pint of rum. For every one hundred men there was to be one quart of salt, two quarts of vinegar, two pounds of soap, and one pound of candles. When government contractors failed to arrive with supplies for the soldiers as Gibson had warned, Jackson ordered Gibson to ship the supplies stored on the southern border in New Orleans "as quickly as possible by the means we agreed necessary to avoid the enemy."

Gibson knew exactly what to do. He loaded the goods on a ship and sent them and his men across the Gulf of Mexico to Apalachicola Bay, Florida. His men then built flat-bottom boats and floated the food upstream to Jackson's forces.

When the quartermaster department was reorganized in 1818, there was no question as to who should be in charge. On April 30, 1818, General George Gibson became the eleventh commissary general of subsistence for the United States. His new policies for providing for the U.S. soldiers reflected Jackson's belief that the only way the nation could be prepared to defend itself was with an army "properly fed, clothed, and sheltered."

For the next forty-three years George Gibson dedicated himself to this effort. He held the position of commissary general longer than any other person. When he died on September 30, 1861, at the age of 87, he was the oldest officer on active duty in the army. He died with a pencil in his hand, preparing a list of supplies for the Union army. He is buried in the Congressional Cemetery in Washington, D.C.

DRUMMERS AND FIFERS

The General sent for me, and told me to play.

—Alexander Milliner, drummer boy for the
Continental army

Whose image is on the back of a 1976 bicentennial (two-hundredth anniversary) commemorative U.S. quarter? It is not the image of a commanding officer, but of a drummer boy wearing a three-cornered hat called a tricorn. Boys and men who played musical instruments were among the most important soldiers of the Revolutionary War. They used fifes (instruments similar to flutes) and drums to sound the signals that told soldiers where and how to fight. They did not always carry weapons and were required to keep playing the commands no matter how heavy the fighting was around them.

General **George Washington** asked **Baron Friedrich von Steuben** to be acting inspector general for his army. Steuben wrote a manual so that all the Continental army soldiers would obey the same orders and regulations. From his experience as a soldier in Europe, Steuben knew that certain notes played by the fife and certain beats of the drum were signals that everyone could understand. Because there was no other means of communicating with the soldiers in a battle, the fifers and drummers were absolutely essential to the commanders. He also knew that British troops used fifes and drums, and he was concerned that the American soldiers would become confused in the midst of fighting about which commands to follow.

The drumheads were made from thick cow skins tied with heavy strings made out of cow intestines. The drummers used heavy, rounded sticks, and the result was a drumbeat that could be heard by soldiers above all the noise of battle. The drum calls Steuben wrote could be used in two ways. A drumbeat was a signal for the whole camp to obey. A drum signal was a command for only a part of the encampment.

Steuben thought that every soldier would play the beats and signals the same. It soon became apparent, however, that not all the drum and fife instructors had been taught the calls and signals the same way. To correct this, Washington, who played the flute, appointed a director of music for the army, who was given the title inspector and superintendent of music. The first person to have this title was Lieutenant John Hiwell, fife instructor in the Third Artillery Regiment. Hiwell had been at Valley Forge, Pennsylvania, with Washington in the winter of 1776–1777. Despite the bitter cold and snow, he made the fifers and drummers practice every day until they all knew the same songs, calls, and signals from memory.

Older boys and sometimes men served as the drummers. The youngest boys served as fifers, because the fifes were not heavy. As a fifer grew older, he would sometimes take over the drum and let a younger boy play the fife. The fifes were about fifteen inches long. Because they were made by hand, each produced a slightly different sound even when the same notes were played on them. Washington ordered the "fife majors" to test the fifes and try to match the tones.

Some fifers joined the army when they were as young as ten years old, but most of the musicians were older. The average age for a drummer was nineteen. The average age for a fifer was seventeen. The calls and signals the fifers and drummers were required to know included the following:

The Drummers' Call was beat by the duty drummer and fifer to assemble the drummers and fifers just before The Reveiller sounded.

The Reveiller, or what we now call *reveille*, was a beat played at dawn that signaled the beginning of the day.

The General was beat instead of the Reveiller if the regiment was to march somewhere.

The March was the beat the troops marched to so that they could keep in step and not lag behind.

The Troop was the beat for the most important formation of the day. It occurred about nine or ten o'clock in the morning and assembled the troops for roll call, inspection, and the day's orders.

The Retreat was beat at sunset for evening roll call and assembly. No drum calls or signals sounded after the Retreat unless there was an alarm.

To Arms was the beat that signaled the soldiers to get their weapons and take their battlefield positions.

The Tattoo was beat at nine o'clock at night in the fall and winter, and at ten o'clock at night in the spring and summer. It was never beat in camp. The Tattoo told local innkeepers they could not sell soldiers any more liquor that day.

Each company had one fifer and one drummer who stood to the right of the first group of soldiers. They sounded and beat whatever command the officers needed the troops to follow. Fifers and drummers were also present anytime a soldier was punished. If a soldier did something dishonorable, he was "drummed" out of the army.

By the end of the Revolutionary War, the need for fifers and drummers had declined. In 1781 Congress decided that the army did not need to enlist people just to play the fife or the drum.

To honor the patriotic fifers and drummers in America's history, the U.S. Army created the Old Guard Fife and Drum Corps in 1960. Assigned to Fort Myers, Virginia, it is the only fife and drum corps in the U.S. armed services.

Only the drum major carries a spontoon. It is a weapon that looks like a spear. It is about six feet long and has a two-edged blade on the top. The drum major carries the spontoon in his right hand and uses it to give silent commands to the rest of the corps. The Drum Major of the Old Guard Fife and Drum Corps is the only soldier in the army today who is allowed to salute with his left hand.

THE ONEIDA

NATIVE AMERICAN PATRIOTS
1775–1815

We fought by your side, our blood flowed together, and the bones of our warriors mingled with yours.

—Chief Hanyery of the Oneida to the U.S. Congress

Tyonajanegen gasped as she watched a musket ball pierce the right wrist of her husband, Chief Hanyery of the Oneida. Hanyery kept fighting with his tomahawk even though he could no longer shoot. Tyonajanegen rode her horse to fight beside him, reloading and firing his gun for him again and again. On August 6, 1777, the Oneida were fighting with the Americans against the British, but some of the men Hanyery and Tyonajanegen killed were not wearing British uniforms. They were Seneca and Mohawk warriors.

Native Americans had formed nations and governments long before Columbus sailed from Spain to the New World. The Oneida were one of six Native American tribes living primarily in what is now New York State that had joined together to form the Iroquois Confederacy. Each tribe sent leaders to a general council that made certain each person in the confederacy received equal justice, while allowing each tribe to govern itself.

In 1758 the British established Fort Stanwix in what is today Rome, New York, offering trade and wealth to the Iroquois in exchange for peace as settlers steadily moved into the Iroquois homelands. As the Revolutionary War moved closer, the six tribes that formed the Iroquois Confederacy split. The Mohawk, the Cayuga, the Onondaga, and the Seneca chose to side with the British because the British had a better supply system and promised to protect the Iroquois land boundaries; the Oneida and the Tuscarora sided with the colonists because they shared the colonists' desire for liberty and independence. They also believed life with the colonists would be better than life under the British when the war was over. "The love of our land which gave us birth supported our resolution," stated Lagwilondonwas, one of the Oneida leaders. Personal issues, however, also influenced the Oneida's choice.

Hanyery (Tehawenkaragwen was his Indian name), the Oneida chief warrior of the Wolf Clan, and Thayendanegea, known as Joseph Brant, a Mohawk chief of the Wolf Clan, were on opposite sides of an angry land dispute. Brant's older sister was married to the Royal Indian Superintendent, so Brant enjoyed favors from the British. Others in the Iroquois Confederation, including Hanyery, believed the British were unfair in the way they ruled the valley the tribes had shared for thousands of years.

The dispute between Hanyery and Brant became so bitter that Hanyery moved his family away from the area and started the Indian village of Oriska (now Oriskany) in the Mohawk Valley of New York. Early in the Revolutionary War, Hanyery formed a militia (citizen soldiers) unit of Oneida at Oriska.

The British planned to surround New England, cutting it off from the rest of the colonies. When the leaders of the Continental army learned of this plan, they were determined to stop the British from dividing the colonies. The sent General Nicholas Herkimer and his army to Fort Stanwix to defeat the British army there. Although the Americans now held the fort, the British had surrounded it.

The Continental army camped in Oriska, eight miles east of Fort Stanwix, on the evening of August 5, 1777. Herkimer asked for volunteers to sneak through the British lines and get inside the fort to let the Americans there know the army was coming to help them. Once safely inside the fort, they were to fire three cannon shots to let the American militia know they were ready to fight. One of the men who volunteered was Adam Helmer, the fastest runner in the Mohawk Valley.

On the morning of August 6, the Continental army waited and waited but heard no cannon shot. The men became restless and accused Herkimer of being a coward. He angrily raised his sword and yelled for his army to advance without organizing the troops. He did not know that was what the British and their Seneca and Mohawk allies were waiting for.

Suddenly there were Mohawk and Seneca everywhere, shooting muskets and fighting with tomahawks, knives, and spears. The Americans were surrounded, but they fought back bravely, with Hanyery leading the Oneida charge.

Though badly wounded, General Herkimer moved his troops to the top of a hill, where they finally had the advantage. The Seneca and Mohawk realized they could not keep fighting. When they heard firing from Fort Stanwix, they yelled *"Oonah! Oonah!"* ("Retreat! Retreat!") and vanished as quickly as they had appeared. The battle had lasted six hours, with many colonists and Oneida dying together, but it saved the Mohawk Valley from invasion by the British. Hanyery and his Oneida militia had helped stop the British from separating New England from the rest of the colonies.

"While the sun and moon continue to give light to the world, we shall love and respect you. As our trusty friends, we shall protect you; and shall at all times consider your welfare as our own," the Continental Congress told the Oneida in 1777.

Later, during the horrible winter of 1777–1778, General **George Washington** and twelve thousand men were stranded and starving at Valley Forge, Pennsylvania. A band of Oneida brought six hundred bushels of corn to them. One Oneida woman, Polly Cooper, showed the troops how to prepare the corn so that they could make more food with it. Martha Washington, wife of General George Washington, gave her a shawl and a bonnet as a way of saying thank you. The shawl remains a treasured part of Oneida history and is displayed on special occasions at the Oneida Cultural Center in Oneida, New York.

After the war ended, the other tribes in the Iroquois Confederacy were angry with the Oneida. They destroyed Oriska and drove the Oneida out of the land they had lived in. Hanyery died in 1794, the year the U.S. government finally signed a treaty with the Oneida promising them possession and control of six million acres in New York for helping win the War of Independence.

Tragically, New York State ignored the federal treaty. Instead, New York made its own treaties with the Oneida after the Revolutionary War, taking all but thirty-two acres away from them. By 1838 many of the Oneida had relocated to Wisconsin and Canada. The U.S. Supreme Court has since ruled twice that the New York State treaties with the Oneida were illegal.

When the Revolutionary War began, there were approximately twelve thousand Iroquois in America. By the end of the war, there were only eight thousand. The war cost the Iroquois not only their lives, families, homes, and land, but also the liberty and independence that they had helped the Americans win.

Dr. Anthony Wonderley, a historian for the Oneida nation, says the Oneida "have always volunteered to fight on behalf of the American government." The Iroquois Confederacy's declaration of war in July 1813 states: "We do hereby command and advise all the War Chiefs to call forth immediately their warriors under them to put them in motion to protect their rights and liberties which our brethren the Americans are now defending." The government of the United States mostly ignored their contributions in the War of 1812, and the Oneida shared in the losses all Native Americans experienced due to the government's unfair policies, treaties, and treatment during the century that followed.

The Oneida are now recognized as a sovereign (self-governed) Indian nation. They are proud that they have kept true to the words spoken to the colonists in 1778 by Lagwilondonwas: ". . . we are determined to adhere to you."

THE DECLARATION
OF INDEPENDENCE

BIRTH CERTIFICATE OF THE NATION
1776–PRESENT

We mutually pledge to each other our Lives, our Fortunes, and our sacred Honor.

—The Declaration of Independence

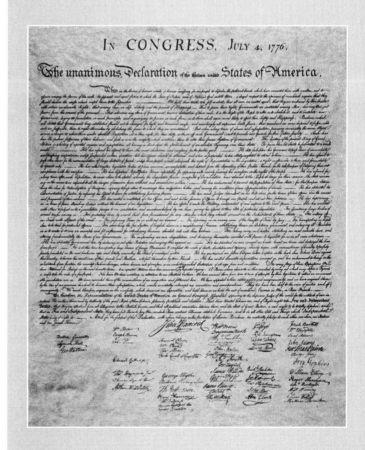

On June 7, 1776, **Richard Henry Lee** introduced a resolution (strong statement of opinion or intent) before the men of the Second Continental Congress: "Resolved, That these United Colonies are, and of right ought to be, free and independent states . . ."

A hush fell over the room where the delegates (representatives) of the thirteen colonies had been meeting in secret. At last the idea they had whispered, argued about, and debated over for months had been put into words and formally announced.

Five delegates—**Roger Sherman**, Robert Livingston, **Thomas Jefferson, John Adams**, and **Benjamin Franklin**—were assigned the job of writing the formal document declaring the United States to be a free and independent nation. During the weeks that followed, Franklin, Adams, and Sherman contributed ideas while Jefferson did most of the actual writing. Livingston, who felt it was too early for the declaration, went back to New York. He later helped negotiate the purchase of the Louisiana Territory from France in 1803.

Jefferson divided the document into three sections. The first section is a statement about the rights of all people and the reasons for revolution; the second section is a list of grievances (complaints) against the British king, George III; the third section is the actual declaration announcing independence.

With the help of **Charles Thomson**, secretary of the Continental Congress, the first draft of the declaration was read to the delegates on June 28. Congress debated, revised, debated, and revised again. On July 2, 1776, a vote in favor of independence was taken. After more revisions, the delegates from twelve of the thirteen colonies adopted the Declaration of Independence on July 4, 1776. **John Hancock**, president of the Continental Congress, signed his name with a swirl and a flourish. Thomson added his signature as a witness. No one else signed the document before Thomson carried it that evening to the printer John Dunlap. Copies called broadsides were printed for the delegates to take home with them. The declaration was soon read in churches and at assemblies, and some newspapers dared to print the document.

On July 15 New York joined the other colonies and made the Declaration of Independence unanimous. Timothy Matlock was asked to engross the declaration. An engrosser used a quill pen to write in large, readable letters on parchment. Parchment was usually made from the thin lining of the stomach of a sheep or a goat.

On August 2 the delegates began signing the engrossed copy, which measured 24 ½ inches by 29 ¾ inches. One week later the signatures of fifty-six men filled the parchment. Hancock centered his bold signature below the last words of the text. The other delegates' signatures started on the right and ended on the left in the order of their state's location. The New Hampshire delegates began the list, and the Georgia delegates ended it. Some of the men who had voted to declare independence on July 4 never signed the final document.

The parchment then traveled wherever the Continental Congress was meeting. It rode in saddlebags and in wagons and was even rolled and stuffed inside boots. Hundreds of hands touched it, and it was often exposed to bright sunlight and moisture. By 1820 the signed Declaration of Independence was in such poor condition that **John Quincy Adams**, then secretary of state, appointed a printer named William J. Stone to make exact copies using a process called wet-ink transfer. Ink from the document was transferred onto a copper plate. The plate was then engraved along the ink lines. It took more than three years to make the copper plate of the Declaration of Independence. Two hundred and one copies were made from this plate in 1823.

The plate was slightly altered and used again in 1848 to make about one thousand copies on rice paper. The plate was not used again until 1976, when a limited number of copies were printed for the two-hundredth anniversary of the United States of America. The copper plate is kept in a special vault at the National Archives in Washington, D.C., and will not be used to print copies again until the year 2076, when the country celebrates its three-hundredth anniversary.

The first document signed by Hancock and witnessed by Thomson on July 4, 1776, was lost. Only a few of the broadsides made from it still exist. Each is worth approximately ten million dollars. The original copy of the Declaration of Independence with the fifty-six signatures did not stop traveling after the Revolutionary War. It has been displayed in various locations, and during World War II it was kept in a vault in Fort Knox, Kentucky. Different pages of the thin, faded parchment are now exhibited in the Rotunda of the National Archives building in Washington, D.C., in a glass case that's filled with helium to prevent decay.

The fifty-six men who signed the Declaration of Independence knew they had signed the birth certificate of a new nation. They also knew they were possibly signing their own death warrants, because the British would consider them traitors. They risked losing their families, homes, businesses, property, and even their lives. By the time the Revolutionary War ended, some had paid with their lives, and many no longer had fortunes. Not one lost his sacred honor.

The names of the signers of the Declaration of Independence

John Hancock	merchant	1737–1793
Josiah Bartlett	doctor	1729–1795
William Whipple	shipbuilder	1730–1785
Matthew Thornton	surgeon	1714–1803
Samuel Adams	lawyer	1722–1803
John Adams	lawyer	1735–1826
Robert Treat Paine	lawyer	1731–1814
Elbridge Gerry	merchant	1744–1814
Stephen Hopkins	lawyer	1707–1785
William Ellery	lawyer	1727–1820
Roger Sherman	lawyer	1721–1793
Samuel Huntington	lawyer	1731–1811
William Williams	merchant	1731–1811
Oliver Wolcott	doctor	1726–1797
Button Gwinnett	farmer	1735–1777
Lyman Hall	doctor	1724–1790
George Walton	lawyer, carpenter	1740–1804
Samuel Chase	lawyer	1741–1811
William Paca	legislator	1740–1799
Thomas Stone	lawyer	1743–1787
Charles Carroll	lawyer	1737–1832
George Wythe	judge	1726–1806

Richard Henry Lee	legislator	1732–1794
Thomas Jefferson	lawyer	1743–1826
Benjamin Harrison	farmer	c.1726–91
Thomas Nelson Jr.	farmer	1738–1789
Francis Lightfoot Lee	farmer	1713–1797
Carter Braxton	farmer	1736–1797
William Floyd	farmer	1734–1821
Philip Livingston	merchant	1716–1778
Francis Lewis	merchant	1713–1802
Lewis Morris	farmer	1726–1798
Robert Morris	merchant	1734–1806
Benjamin Rush	doctor	1745–1813
Benjamin Franklin	printer	1706–1790
John Morton	judge	1724–1777
George Clymer	merchant	1739–1813
James Smith	lawyer	c.1719–1806
George Taylor	ironmaster	1716–1781
James Wilson	lawyer	1742–1798
George Ross	lawyer	1730–1779
Caesar Rodney	public official	1728–1783
George Read	lawyer	1733–1798
Thomas McKean	lawyer	1734–1817
William Hooper	lawyer	1742–1790
Joseph Hewes	merchant	1730–1779
John Penn	lawyer	1741–1788
Edward Rutledge	lawyer	1749–1800
Thomas Heyward	Jr., lawyer	1746–1809
Thomas Lynch	Jr., lawyer	1749–1779
Arthur Middleton	farmer	1742–1787
Richard Stockton	lawyer	1730–1781
John Witherspoon	clergyman	1723–1794
Francis Hopkinson	lawyer	1737–1791
John Hart	farmer	c.1711–1779
Abraham Clark	lawyer	1725–1794

DAUGHTERS OF LIBERTY

WOMEN WHO SERVED IN THE REVOLUTIONARY WAR 1776–1783

I shall not go to that cellar should the enemy come. I will take a spear, which I can use as well as any man, and help defend the fort.

—Mary Hagidorn

The names of many brave women and the stories of their patriotic deeds were not included in most of the official Revolutionary War military records. They were, however, recorded in local histories, diaries, and family Bibles.

Phoebe Anderson of Pennsylvania requested a soldier's pension (money paid for past services) on February 18, 1825. At that time she was ninety-three years of age. Her request stated that she deserved the pension because she "accompanied her husband in the Continental army throughout the whole war." In addition to cooking and cleaning in the army camps, Anderson "assisted in picking up balls thrown from the enemy's cannon." The Americans then used the cannonballs to fire back at the British.

Anne Warner Bailey earned the title "the Heroine of Groton" because of her aid to the wounded after a massacre at Fort Griswold near New London, Connecticut. In addition to going from house to house gathering bandages for the soldiers, she walked three miles to the fort in search of her uncle. She found him seriously wounded. He asked to see his wife and baby before he died, so Bailey went back for them and brought them safely to him.

There are many stories of women patriots who were kind to the wounded enemy. A Connecticut woman known as Mrs. Butterfield discovered a bleeding British officer in her home. Even though she was condemned for it, she cared for him for ten days until he died. "Only a coward would kill a dying man," she said.

On December 2, 1777, Lydia Darragh listened outside the door as the British, meeting in her parlor, planned a surprise attack on General **George Washington**'s army at Whitemarsh, thirteen miles northwest of Philadelphia, for the following day. Doubly alarmed because her son was a soldier at Whitemarsh, Darragh managed to pass through British lines the next day, pretending to buy flour at a nearby mill. She began a sixteen-mile walk through the snow to warn the endangered men. She met an American officer on horseback who delivered her message with all the details of the planned attack. Her message saved her son, General Washington, and Washington's army from disaster.

Margaret Kemble Gage was an American colonist married to Boston's British military governor. She is believed to have provided information to the Americans before the battle at Concord, New Hampshire's, North Bridge.

Seventy-one-year-old Martha Moulton scolded the invading British soldiers who were burning captured supplies in Concord. They had set the roof of the Town House on fire. When she finally persuaded them to put out the blaze, Americans who were camped nearby saw the smoke and marched to the town's rescue.

Rebecca Barrett, the wife of an American militia (citizen soldier) colonel, hid military supplies on the family farm when the British came there to camp. Her fifteen-year-old granddaughter, Meliscent, persuaded a British officer to teach her how to roll powder (charges) for musket shot. As soon as the British left, she organized a group of young women to help make powder charges that they then smuggled to the militia.

Angelica Vrooman sat in a tent in Connecticut and calmly molded shot (bullets) for the patriot muskets. Outside the tent the battle between the British and the colonists raged. When Angelica heard the cry, "More shot!" she would slip out of the tent and carry the shot to the soldiers.

Prudence Cummings became captain of a military company that patrolled her town. She is credited with capturing a British officer.

Nancy Hart lived on Wild Woman Creek in Georgia near the Broad River Settlement. When British soldiers discovered the Hart cabin, they ordered Nancy to fix them a meal. She kept them occupied by providing them food and drink until her husband and son returned. According to family history the Harts killed the soldiers and buried them beneath the cabin.

Rachel and Grace Martin used their knowledge of the countryside to string lines across roads where British couriers (messengers) traveled. When a courier's horse would trip on the string and throw its rider off, the women, disguised as men, would grab the horse and ride away with whatever was in the saddlebags!

At a time when a woman in America could not own property in her own name, attend most public schools, or vote in any election, these and countless other daughters of liberty helped to win the Revolutionary War. They also set the stage for the woman suffrage movement in the United States.

THE CULPER RING

MASTER SPIES OF THE AMERICAN REVOLUTION 1778–1783

*S*ir. Dqpeu Beyocpu agreeable to 28 met 723 not far from 727 and received a 356.

—Beginning of a coded letter sent by Aaron Woodhull, alias Samuel Culper Sr.

General **George Washington** was the most trusted patriot of the American Revolution. But whom could Washington trust to be his spies when the British occupied New York City?

As early as 1775, the Continental Congress set up the Committee of Secret Correspondence to communi-

Benjamin Tallmadge, leader of the Culper Ring spy network

cate in cipher (code) with agents and ministers in Europe. **Benjamin Franklin** developed some of the early codes using numbers for letters of the alphabet. As more and more messages were captured, codes became more difficult to create, and new methods to conceal messages were invented.

Dr. James Jay, the brother of patriot **John Jay**, was living in England when he began providing "sympathetic stain," an ink he invented, to his brother for the Americans to use. Jay's invisible ink was made of cobalt chloride, glycerin, and water. It became visible when exposed to certain kinds of heat. Messages would be written on a blank piece of paper that was then placed between other sheets of paper. The receiver of the papers would know how many sheets to count down to get to the "blank" page that contained the secret message written in the invisible ink. Messages were also written between the lines and spaces of another printed document.

Both the Americans and the British passed laws stating that anyone caught spying to help the enemy would be hanged. In 1778 Washington ordered his spymaster, Benjamin Tallmadge, to organize a group that could pass coded messages to him in Connecticut about the British troops, supplies, and plans in New York. Tallmadge, who used the name "John Bolton," had been a school-teacher in Connecticut when the Revolutionary War broke out.

Aaron Woodhull volunteered to be part of Tallmadge's spy ring. Woodhull's family farm was in Setauket, across Long Island Sound from Connecticut. He was given the code name "Samuel Culper Sr." Robert Townsend, a successful merchant who had convinced the British army he was loyal to Britain, became "Samuel Culper Jr."

Tallmadge created an elaborate code known only to himself, Woodhull, Townsend, and General Washington. Tallmadge prepared four code books, assigning numbers to words that appeared in a common dictionary of the day. Names and places were also given numbers: Washington was 711; Tallmadge was 721; Townsend was 723; New York was 727.

Spies such as Enoch Hale, brother of **Nathan Hale**, helped feed information to Townsend. Hale hated the British because they had hanged his brother for spying two years earlier. Other members of the Culper Ring were Austin Roe, the supervisor of Townsend's mule-pack trains; Caleb Brewster, a farmer with a rowboat; and Anna Strong, whose husband had been taken captive by the British. Tallmadge wrote most of the messages using invisible ink. Even if the other spies could have read the messages, they would not have known what they said, because they did not have copies of the code book.

The ring worked like this: Culper Jr. (Townsend) would take the information he gathered to Austin Roe, who would deliver the message to Culper Sr., (Woodhull), who would pass the message on to Caleb Brewster, who would get it to Bolton (Tallmadge), who would deliver the message to Washington in Connecticut. When Washington wanted to get a message to Townsend in New York, the process was reversed. Anna Strong hung black petticoats on her clothesline as a signal to Brewster when a message needed to be picked up from one of the coves along the shore. The number of handkerchiefs on her clothesline identified which cove he should row to.

The system allowed Townsend to present Washington with an accurate report each day on British headquarters' activities. Townsend reported information about warships coming into and out of the harbor, and he warned Washington about those who claimed to be patriots who were actually supporting the British. Washington was also able to feed false information to the British that helped him delay their plans while he regrouped his troops.

The Culper Ring was never detected. After the war Washington ordered that all records of the ring be sealed to ensure no harm ever came to the spies.

It wasn't until 1939 that the historian and researcher Morton Pennypacker revealed the Culper code for the first time. As recently as 1998, Dr. Jay's formulas for invisible ink were considered classified information by the Central Intelligence Agency.

"THE STAR-SPANGLED BANNER"

THE NATIONAL ANTHEM OF THE UNITED STATES OF AMERICA
1780–PRESENT

Does not such a country . . . deserve a song?

—Francis Scott Key

Anthems are words set to music that unite individuals and make them feel part of a group. The British organist John Stafford Smith, the seamstress Mary Young Pickersgill, and the American lawyer Francis Scott Key never thought that their combined

Francis Scott Key, creator of the national anthem, watches British Forces attack Fort McHenry.

talents would produce the song that was adopted in 1931 as the national anthem of the United States of America.

Smith, born in 1750, was a choirboy at the Chapel Royal London before becoming an outstanding organist at England's Gloucester Cathedral. He composed beautiful and serious music and was elected a member of the elite Anachreonic Society, named for a sixth-century Greek poet and musician. Smith also had a sense of humor. In 1780 he composed the words and music to a song titled "To Anachreon in Heaven," a fun piece about the pleasures of wine and love.

Mary Young Pickersgill was born in 1776, the year the colonies declared independence. By 1813 she was a widow living at 44 Queen Street (now 844 East Pratt Street) in Baltimore. A banner by her door advertised "Silk Standards & Cavalry Colours, and other Colours of Every Description." Pickersgill was a successful businesswoman well known for making ships' flags. The United States of America was at war with the British, and Commander George Armistead sent an order to Pickersgill for a flag "so large that the British [would] have no difficulty in seeing it from a distance."

Pickersgill's mother had sewn flags for General **George Washington** during the Revolutionary War. Now Pickersgill, her mother, her thirteen-year-old daughter, and her two nieces went to work. They gathered eight-inch-wide strips of lightweight wool fabric called bunting. These strips had to be sewn together to make each of the seven white stripes and eight red stripes two feet wide. The fifteen stars representing the fifteen states were made from cotton. Each star measured two feet from top to bottom.

The Pickersgill home was not large enough to lay out a flag the size the general had ordered, so Pickersgill went to nearby Claggett's Brewery, where she was given permission to spread the flag on the floor to stitch it. Every stitch in every star and seam was made by hand over a period of six weeks. The flag, forty-two feet long and thirty feet high, was delivered to Fort McHenry, Maryland, on August 19, 1813. The U.S. government paid Pickersgill $405.90 for the work. This would be more than $4,000 today.

Francis Scott Key was born in 1779. Key, a respected young lawyer, and Colonel John Skinner, an American agent for prisoner-of-war exchanges, were themselves prisoners of the British. They had boarded a British ship hoping to obtain the release of an elderly American doctor. The British refused to release the three men until the British completed their attack on Fort McHenry.

At seven A.M. on September 13, 1814, the British began their bombardment of Fort McHenry. All day and through the night the helpless Key tried to keep his sight focused on the huge flag flying over the fort while hundreds of 220-pound bombs exploded. As long as the flag was flying, he knew the Americans had not surrendered. When the cannon fire stopped during the night, Key feared the British had won, but in the first rays of sunlight the next morning, he caught a glimpse of the Stars and Stripes, waving through the smoke and rain. Overwhelmed by the sight, he took a letter out of his pocket and, using his best skills as an amateur poet, began to write on the back of it:

Oh, say can you see, by the dawn's early light . . .

On and on Key wrote, inspired by the sight of the American flag still waving after twenty-five hours of attack. After returning to Baltimore, he completed all the verses of the poem and gave a copy to his brother-in-law, who took it to a printer, who published it as "The Defense of Fort McHenry." It appeared in the September 20, 1814, issue of *The Baltimore Patriot*. Other newspapers soon printed it as well, saying it filled hearts with "the patriotic spirit" all Americans should be proud to share.

One newspaper suggested that the words fit the rhythm of a song Americans already knew, "To Anachreon in Heaven." On October 19, 1814, a theater actor sang the combination of Smith's tune and Key's words as "The Star-Spangled Banner" for the first time before a large crowd. The military service bands quickly added it to their performances, and its popularity increased. The U.S.

Marine Corps began referring to it in their performances as "the national anthem."

John Stafford Smith, who died in 1836, was pleased that the words Key wrote were sung to his music. An American flag flies every day at his grave in Gloucester, England.

Mary Young Pickersgill used part of the money she earned making the Fort McHenry flag to start a charitable society to help other widows. She died in 1857. The flag she made that flew over Fort McHenry is in the Smithsonian Institution in Washington, D.C., where it has recently undergone an eighteen-million-dollar restoration.

Francis Scott Key wrote other poems, but none as famous as his words to the national anthem. He died in 1843. An American flag flies continuously over his grave in Frederick, Maryland, and a flag also flies continuously over old Fort McHenry.

The United States officially adopted "The Star-Spangled Banner" as its national anthem on March 3, 1931. In the years since some groups have tried to have Congress designate a different song as the national anthem, but so far none have succeeded.

THE PURPLE HEART

he road to glory in a patriot army and a free country is open to all.

—General George Washington, general orders of August 7, 1782

The Continental Congress made itself very clear in a message sent to General **George Washington** in the summer of 1782: Washington was ordered to stop rewarding common soldiers with money or advanced rank.

Regardless of how brave or courageous these soldiers' deeds in combat may have been, Congress explained, there were no funds to pay for these rewards: "You must find another way to recognize the loyalty and service of your troops."

No one appreciated the contributions of the ordinary soldiers of the Revolutionary War more than Washington. After he received the order, he struggled with the problem of what to do. If money and rank could not be given as rewards, what could he substitute?

The solution Washington came up with in 1782 was used briefly, then was forgotten for 150 years. Discovered among the War Department records was an order written by Washington that read in part: ". . . the General . . . directs that whenever any singularly meritorious action is performed, the author of it shall be permitted to wear . . . over his left breast, the figure of a heart in purple cloth . . ."

The order Washington had issued went on to state that in addition to wearing the purple heart, the person's name should be enrolled in a "Book of Merit." No such book has been found from the Revolutionary War period; however, the names of the first three soldiers who received what was then known as the Badge of Military Merit in 1783 were with the copy of the order. Elijah Churchill received the award for gallantry in action at Fort St. George at Coram, New York. William Brown received the award, possibly in recognition for his service and courage at the Battle of Yorktown in New York. Daniel Bissell Jr. received the award for pretending to be a deserter. This placed him in double danger from both the British and the Americans, who did not know that he was acting as a spy under direct orders of Washington.

The Badge of Military Merit was not used after the Revolutionary War until General Douglas MacArthur pushed through efforts to have it reinstated. The War Department announced the award, now called the Purple Heart, in General Order No. 3 on February 22, 1932:

"By order of the President of the United States, the Purple Heart established by General George Washington at Newburgh, August 7, 1782, during the War of Revolution, is hereby revived out of respect to his memory and military achievements."

Elizabeth Will was named to redesign the newly revived medal. Will, an army artist who specialized in creating symbolic decorations, used Washington's written description to make the sketch for the current medal of the Purple Heart. It consists of a purple heart made of metal, not cloth, within a bronze border showing a profile of George Washington in his Continental army uniform. The medal is less than two inches in length and is held by a purple band with white borders. The process of transforming the rough heart stamped from bronze to the finished medal requires nineteen steps.

The definition of who is entitled to receive the Purple Heart has been revised through the years. It is now awarded to any person wounded in action while serving in any of the armed forces of the United States of America. It is also presented to the next of kin of a person killed in action or who died of wounds received in action.

The record of the first person to receive the Purple Heart after it was revived in 1932 cannot be found. Thousands of recipients since then have considered the Purple Heart one of their most cherished awards. According to the Miltiary Order of the Purple Heart, an organization founded to assist needy and disabled soldiers, "it is the oldest military decoration in the world in present use and the first award made available to a common soldier."

Nothing would have pleased George Washington more.

ZACHARY TAYLOR

PATRIOT PRESIDENT WHO HELD THE
UNION TOGETHER
1784–1850

I have nothing to serve but my country.

—Zachary Taylor, April 22, 1848

Margaret Taylor smiled as she watched her stocky, gray-haired husband put on his formal attire on the morning of March 5, 1849. After thirty-eight years of marriage to Zachary Taylor, she was certain he would much rather wear his wide-brimmed straw hat and his mismatched coat and pants for his inauguration as president of the United States of America.

When Zachary Taylor took the oath as the twelfth president, he became the first career soldier to hold that office. He also became the first president who had not fought in the Revolutionary War or served in the Continental Congress.

Taylor was born on November 24, 1784, in Virginia, one of nine children born to Richard and Sarah Dabney Strother Taylor. The family later moved to Kentucky, and Zachary grew up near Louisville. He had no formal schooling, but his parents taught him at home, as was common in what was then frontier territory.

Taylor joined the army in 1808, the year his second cousin, **James Madison**, became president. Zachary married Margaret in 1810 and two years later was an army captain winning distinction for his bravery.

Taylor did not look much like a soldier. He did not wear a military uniform, and when he reviewed his troops, he liked to ride his favorite horse, Old Whitey, with one leg thrown across the saddle horn.

Taylor built Fort Texas on the American side of the Rio Grande after Texas became a state. On April 25, 1846, about 1,600 Mexican soldiers surrounded the American soldiers in Fort Texas and killed or captured them. This was the unofficial start of the Mexican War. Several days later Taylor and Mexican general Mariano Arista engaged in two battles, and the Americans won both.

Taylor became a national hero. He attacked Monterrey, Mexico, believing the United States would not be safe without the destruction of the Mexican army. The bloody battle ended when Taylor agreed to let the Mexican army retreat.

Almost a year later, however, Taylor and his troops fell into a trap and were attacked by Mexican general Antonio Lopez de Santa Anna in Buena Vista, Mexico. With an army one-fourth the size of Santa Anna's, Taylor won the battle. This victory also won for him the hearts of the people of the United States.

Taylor thought of himself as a soldier, not a politician. He did not know that the Whig political party had nominated him as its presidential candidate. The party secretary sent him a notice of his nomination by mail without enough postage, and Taylor refused to accept the letter. After the secretary put on more stamps and resent the letter, Taylor learned he was their candidate.

The $25,000 a year that Taylor would earn as president was far more than he had earned in his years as a soldier and cotton farmer. Yet the money did not make Margaret happy to move into the White House.

"I have no interest in the duties of First Lady," Margaret told her daughter, Betty Taylor Bliss.

"Then I will do them for you while Papa is busy keeping the union together," her daughter assured her.

After the Taylors moved into the White House, Margaret was seldom seen by anyone other than her family. The president especially enjoyed having his children and grandchildren with him there. When friends came to visit, he gave them hairs from Old Whitey as souvenirs.

Taylor owned slaves, so the Southerners liked him. He did not believe slavery should extend to any new states, so the Northerners liked him. Above all, Taylor was a nationalist who believed his country had to stay united, and he was willing to do whatever it took to preserve the union.

By 1850 some of President Taylor's opinions had made him unpopular with people on both sides of the slavery dispute. A group of Southern leaders met with him in February and threatened to secede (withdraw) from the United States. Taylor did not hesitate with his rough-and-ready response. He told them that if necessary, he would personally lead the U.S. Army to stop them: "I will hang any person taken in rebellion against the union."

Zachary Taylor was a man who spoke with simplicity. Many presidents have quoted the words that have come to define him as the patriot president who held the union together: ". . . kingdoms and empires have fallen, (but) this union has stood unshaken. The patriots who formed it have long since descended to the grave; yet still it remains, the proudest monument to their memory. Upon its preservation must depend our own happiness and that of countless generations to come. Whatever dangers may threaten it, I shall stand by it and maintain it in its integrity to the full extent of the obligations imposed and the power conferred upon me by the **Constitution of the United States of America**."

Some historians believe there would never have been an American Civil War if Zachary Taylor had not suddenly become ill and died on July 9, 1850. He had been president for little more than a year. When the war did begin eleven years later, his only son, Richard, served as a general . . . in the Confederate army.

THE CONSTITUTION OF THE UNITED STATES OF AMERICA

CHART OF FREEDOM
1787–PRESENT

e, the People . . .

—Preamble of the U.S. Constitution

James Madison looked over the list of names of the men who had arrived in Philadelphia late in May 1787. Their purpose: to revise the Articles of Confederation, which had governed the United States of America since it had won independence from Britain. In actuality, Madison knew, the delegates would be writing a new constitution.

A constitution is a set of rules and laws that tells how a government is organized and run. The Constitution of the United States of America has 4,543 words, including the signatures of the thirty-nine delegates (representatives) from twelve of the thirteen original states (Rhode Island did not send any delegates to the Constitutional Convention).

The delegates met in secret behind windows covered in oiled paper to keep out the flies and dust from the Philadelphia streets. Fifty-five delegates would attend the Constitutional Convention between May and September, though not all were present all of the time. Madison did not miss a single session. **Thomas Jefferson** attended none—he was away in France.

The oldest delegate was eighty-one-year-old **Benjamin Franklin** of Pennsylvania. He had to be carried into each of the sessions on a chair because of his poor health. The youngest delegate was twenty-six-year-old Jonathan Dayton of New Jersey. **George Washington** served as president of the convention for the entire time.

After weeks of extreme debate and argument that almost led to physical violence between delegates, a Committee of Style was selected to prepare the final version of the document. Madison was in charge of the committee. His diary of the convention indicates that much of the actual writing was the work of the Pennsylvania delegate Gouverneur Morris.

Most of the delegates were well educated. At least forty-one of the fifty-five had served some time in Congress. Some had fought in the Revolutionary War; others had never been away from home before. They were lawyers, businessmen, writers, farmers, printers, merchants, doctors—and some, like Franklin, had too many occupations to list.

Jacob Shallus, a former minuteman in the Continental army, had been hired to be the clerk of the Constitutional Convention. Shallus was an engrosser. Using pens cut from large feathers and ink made from oak nuts, iron, and gum, Shallus wrote important legal documents on parchment made from animal skin specially treated with lime and stretched thin. On the evening of September 15, 1787, Shallus was given the job of engrossing the words onto parchment that the delegates had voted to accept as the new Constitution of the United States of America. He had until Monday afternoon, September 17, to write a final copy for the delegates to sign.

When Shallus presented his work to the convention on September 17, it filled four sheets of parchment approximately twenty-nine inches by twenty-three inches each. In some areas words had been scraped away with a penknife to correct mistakes; in other places words had been inserted between the lines of text and then listed in a paragraph to state that the corrections were part of the approved document. Because he had written so much in such a short amount of time, Shallus's hand shook. He was delighted to be finished and hoped he could collect the thirty dollars he had been promised as payment for his services for the summer.

His work was not finished, though. The delegates wanted an introduction—a statement declaring the purpose of the document and to assure the states it would not create a government like the one they had fought to free themselves of. Franklin handed Shallus a note that begin with the three words that have come to identify the nation:

"We, the People . . ." the preamble began.

As plans were being made to celebrate the 150th anniversary of the U.S. Constitution in 1937, a researcher noticed the difference between the handwriting of the preamble and that of the body of the document. Handwriting analysts confirmed that Jacob Shallus was indeed the man who penned the text in the body. Further research has led many to conclude that Jacob's son, Francis Shallus, penned the words of the preamble. Francis was a fourteen-year-old apprentice calligrapher learning the art of engrossing.

Shallus never received payment for his work. The nation with the new Constitution did not have the money to pay its obligations.

Some delegates refused to attend the Constitutional Convention or to sign the document because they wanted more guarantees of individual rights. One delegate, John Dickinson, became ill and had delegate George Read sign for him. Copies were made and sent to each of the states for ratification (acceptance). Nine states were required to accept the Constitution in order for it to become law. On June 21, 1788, New Hampshire became the ninth state. The first Congress under the Constitution met on March 4, 1789.

The Fifth Article of the Constitution wisely provided for a way to amend (change) it to meet the unknown needs of the future. The first ten amendments adopted by Congress on December 15, 1791, are known as the Bill of Rights. Only twenty-seven amendments have been made to the Constitution, including the Bill of Rights.

The original copy of the Constitution is enclosed in an airtight, helium-filled case at the National Archives Building in Washington, D.C.

The thirty-nine signatures on the Constitution are:

George Washington	1732–1799
John Langdon	1741–1819
Nicholas Gilman	1755–1814
Nathaniel Gorham	1738–1796
Rufus King	1755–1827
William Samuel Johnson	1727–1819
Roger Sherman	1721–1793
Alexander Hamilton	1755–1804
William Livingston	1723–1790
David Brearley	1745–1790
William Paterson	1745–1806
Jonathan Dayton	1760–1824
Benjamin Franklin	1706–1790
Thomas Mifflin	1744–1800
Robert Morris	1734–1806

George Clymer	1739–1813
Thomas Fitzsimons	1741–1811
Jared Ingersoll	1749–1822
James Wilson	1741–1796
Gouverneur Morris	1752–1816
George Read	1733–1798
Gunning Bedford Jr.	1747–1812
*John Dickinson	1732–1808
Richard Bassett	1745–1815
Jacob Broom	1752–1810
James McHenry	1723–1816
Daniel of St. Tho. Jenifer	1723–1790
Daniel Carroll	1730–1796
John Blair	1732–1800
James Madison	1751–1836
William Blount	1749–1800
Richard Dobbs Spaight	1758–1802
Hugh Williamson	1735–1819
John Rutledge	1739–1800
Charles Cotesworth Pinckney	1746–1825
Charles Pinckney	1757–1824
Pierce Butler	1744–1822
William Few	1748–1828
Abraham Baldwin	1754–1807

*Name signed by George Read for Dickinson

PUBLIUS

AUTHOR OF *THE FEDERALIST PAPERS*
1787–1788

THE

FEDERALIST:

A COLLECTION

OF

E S S A Y S,

WRITTEN IN FAVOUR OF THE

NEW CONSTITUTION,

AS AGREED UPON BY THE FEDERAL CONVENTION,
SEPTEMBER 17, 1787.

IN TWO VOLUMES.

VOL. I.

NEW-YORK:

PRINTED AND SOLD BY J. AND A. M'LEAN,
No. 41, HANOVER-SQUARE,
M,DCC,LXXXVIII.

The best commentary on the principles of government which has ever been written

—Thomas Jefferson

"Publius" was the pen name used by **Alexander Hamilton, James Madison,** and **John Jay** to write a series of articles supporting the ratification of (agreement to) the **Constitution of the United States of America.** A constitution is a set of rules and laws that say how a government is organized and run. It was not unusual in 1787 for writers of political opinions to publish their articles under pen names. Many of these names, such as Brutus and Caesar, were picked from Roman history. By writing without identifying themselves, the authors could express their views without fear of ridicule or harm.

In 1787 the new nation of the United States of America was in trouble because the government had no money to pay its debts and to protect its citizens, and it had no way to raise money. The states were loosely held together under the Articles of Confederation. While these articles had been helpful in uniting the colonies, they were now contributing to the problems that were dividing the states.

At the urging of **Benjamin Franklin**, **George Washington**, and **James Madison**, a group of delegates (representatives) met in Philadelphia, hoping to revise the articles. When they realized that the Articles of Confederation could not be made to fit the needs of the new nation, some delegates wanted to create a constitution. Others, including the two delegates who came with Alexander Hamilton to represent New York, left. They feared that a new constitution would create a government with more power than the people.

Hamilton himself was reluctant at first. When the final version of the Constitution was presented, however, Hamilton begged to sign it even though it had not been written exactly the way he wanted. He understood how the American people who had just won their independence would be afraid of establishing a strong central government. If people could understand how the Constitution had been written with checks and balances to prevent the loss of individual liberty, Hamilton felt certain they would not listen to "Cato" and "Sydney," writers who were filling the New York newspapers with arguments against ratifying the Constitution.

Hamilton considered writing a series of articles in favor of the Constitution by himself. Then, recognizing that he did not have time to write and still pay off his personal debts, he asked Madison and Jay, the secretary of foreign affairs, to join him. The three men worked together to write a series of articles for newspapers, which they published under the pen name Publius.

The eighty-five essays the men wrote over a period of approximately ten months became known as *The Federalist Papers*. Most of the essays were written quickly in order to meet the deadlines of the newspapers.

Was there a real person named Publius? In 1818 Madison explained that the pen name the three men chose referred to Valerius Publicola, a Roman legislator. He was one of the first republican statesmen who defended the rights of the citizens of ancient Rome. He died in about the fifth century B.C.

By July 1788 Publius had succeeded in persuading the citizens of New York and other states to ratify the Constitution. However, the popularity of *The Federalist Papers* was just beginning. Copies of the documents were soon translated into other languages, and new editions were published and read around the world. The descendants of Hamilton, Madison, and Jay battled bitterly for years over the rights of ownership of the essays. The papers, with commentaries by various scholars, became one of the best-selling collections of writing in the world. They are still published and studied by legal scholars hoping to understand the thinking of the writers of the Constitution.

The identity of the author of each essay is still debated: Madison and Hamilton both claimed authorship of several of the articles; Jay is believed to have written only five. What is not debated is the worth of the Constitution of the United States of America. It continues to provide the foundation for a republic with a democratic system of government that is unequaled in the world.

SAM HOUSTON

THE RAVEN WHO REFUSED TO SECEDE
1793–1863

I would lay down my life to defend any one of the States from aggression.

—Sam Houston

Sam Houston had fought with **Andrew Jackson** in the War of 1812, led Texas to win independence from Mexico, been elected president of the Republic of Texas, and helped Texas become the twenty-eighth state in the union. Yet the battle ahead of him in his sixty-eighth year would be more difficult than any of those he'd previously fought. Governor Houston had to convince the members of the Texas legislature meeting in a special session not to secede (withdraw) Texas from the union.

"I have always been a Southern man for the union," he told his wife, Margaret. "I cannot bear the thought of the blood secession will spill on the very soil I have bled to unite."

The Revolutionary War had ended only ten years before Samuel Houston was born on March 2, 1793, in Virginia, the fifth of nine children. His parents, Samuel and Elizabeth Houston, wanted him to get a complete education, but young Sam was interested only in learning to read. His father died when he was thirteen, and the next year Elizabeth moved the family to Tennessee. When Houston was fifteen, he decided he did not want to work on the family farm or in the family store, so he ran away to live with the Cherokee people. Chief Oolooteka (also known as John Jolly) adopted him and gave him the Indian name *Colonneh*, or "the Raven." Houston credited Oolooteka as the person most responsible for teaching him leadership, bravery, and public-speaking skills.

Houston left the Cherokee when he was eighteen and established a country school in Tenneesee. He needed money to pay off a debt, so he charged each student eight dollars to attend for one term. One-third of the payment had to be in cash, one-third in corn, and one-third in cloth that could be made into shirts. People laughed at the six-foot, two-inch teenager, but the school proved to be a success. Many years later he said this experience gave him "a higher feeling of dignity and self-satisfaction than from any office or honor I have since held."

Houston enlisted to fight the British during the War of 1812. He served under General Andrew Jackson and with the Cherokee warrior **Sequoyah** at the Battle of Horseshoe Bend near what is now Daviston, Alabama, in March of 1814. He was wounded three times and was left to die. The battle put an end to the problems with the Upper Creek Indians, who had joined with the British to fight against the Americans.

After he resigned from the army, Houston studied law and opened a legal practice not far from the home of Andrew Jackson in Tennessee. Jackson helped Houston get elected to Congress in 1823. Four years later at the age of thirty-four, Houston was elected governor of Tennessee.

In 1829 Houston married eighteen-year-old Eliza Allen. The marriage ended after eleven weeks, and Houston abruptly resigned his office and moved west. He went back to the home of Chief Oolooteka in what is now Oklahoma. For the next three years he dressed like his Cherokee family and avoided everyone he had known back east except his friend Andrew Jackson. This time the nickname the Cherokee gave him was "Big Drunk." He married a part-Cherokee, Tiara (Diana) Rogers Gentry, under Cherokee law, and established a trading post.

Houston eventually left Tiara (their marriage was dissolved under Cherokee law) and went to Texas, which was still part of Mexico at the time. He opened a law practice in Nacogdoches, where he obtained a divorce from his first wife, Eliza, in 1837. Everyone living in Texas at that time was required to become a member of the Catholic Church. Houston was given yet another name when he was baptized as Samuel Pablo.

By October 1835 Houston believed that Texas would have to fight to win independence from Mexico. He became the commander of volunteers from Nacogdoches to begin what he called the "work of liberty." In November he became major general of the Texas army.

In March 1836 Houston was a delegate (representative) to the convention where the Texas Declaration of Independence was adopted on March 2. Houston and his "Texian" army now faced the larger, better-prepared army of General Antonio Lopez de Santa Anna. General Santa Anna massacred the Texan troops at the Alamo mission near San Antonio and at the presidio (fort) at Goliad. At the decisive Battle of San Jacinto on April 21, 1836, Houston defeated Santa Anna's army. Six months later Houston was elected the first president of the Republic of Texas. He won the Texas presidency again in 1841 and served until December 1844.

In 1840 Houston married twenty-one-year-old Margaret Lea of Marion, Alabama. The couple had eight children.

When Texas became a state in December 1845, Houston was elected a senator. His greatest concern was the growing conflicts between the different sections of the country over slavery and the rights of the states. He desperately wanted unity, but his opinions and responses to the problems made him unpopular with both pro-slavery and antislavery groups.

Houston returned to Texas and was elected governor in 1859. A year later he met defeat in his effort to win the presidential nomination of the Union Party. This was one of many defeats Houston had faced in his life, but it would not be the worst. That came on March 4, 1861, when Texas seceded from the United States despite Houston's efforts.

To remain governor after Texas seceded, Houston had to take the oath of loyalty to the newly formed Confederate States of America. "I refuse to take this oath," he told the legislators. Rather than bring more bloodshed to Texas, Houston stepped aside and allowed a new governor to take his place. According to Houston's descendant Mary Louise Teasdale, "This experience had a profound impact on my great-grandfather and influenced his later decision to sacrifice his position of power. He believed the destruction of the union would be worse than death."

He returned to his home in Huntsville, Texas, where he died of pneumonia on July 26, 1863. He is buried in Oakwood Cemetery at Huntsville. Nearby Sam Houston State University honors the man who said, "Give to the rising generation instruction."

TO FIND OUT MORE

BOOKS

General

Borneman, Walter. *1812: The War That Forged a Nation*. New York: HarperCollins, 2004.

Brooks, Philip. *Extraordinary Jewish Americans*. New York: Children's Press, 1998.

Countryman, Edward. *The American Revolution*, revised ed. New York: Hill & Wang, 2003.

Gallagher, Mary A. Y. *The American Revolution: A Short History*. Melbourne, FL: Krieger Publishing, 2001.

Grant, George. *The Patriot's Handbook: A Citizenship Primer for a New Generation of Americans*, 2nd ed. Nashville, TN: Cumberland House Publishing, 2004.

Kennedy, Caroline. *A Patriot's Handbook: Songs, Poems, Stories and Speeches Celebrating the Land We Love*. New York: Hyperion, 2003.

Kneib, Martha. *Women Soldiers, Spies, and Patriots of the American Revolution* (American Women at War). New York: Rosen Publishing Group, 2004.

Mitchell, Joseph B. *Decisive Battles of the American Revolution*. Yardley, PA: Westholme Publishing, 2004.

Othow, Helen Chavis; Muhammad, Benjamin F. *John Chavis: African American Patriot, Preacher, Teacher, and Mentor (1783–1838)*. Jefferson, NC: McFarland & Co., 2001.

Raphael, Ray. *A People's History of the American Revolution: How Common People Shaped the Fight for Independence*. New York: Perennial, 2002.

Ridpath, John Clark. *Memorable Addresses by American Patriots*. Patrick Henry University Press, 2001.

Rhodehamel, John. *The American Revolution: Writings from the War of Independence*. New York: Library of America, 2001.

Unger, Harlow Giles. *John Hancock: Merchant King and American Patriot*. New York: Wiley, 2000.

Wood, Gordon S. *The American Revolution: A History* (Modern Library Chronicles). New York: Modern Library, 2002.

The Declaration of Independence
Freedman, Russell. *Give Me Liberty: The Story of the Declaration of Independence.* New York: Holiday House, 2000.

Dolley Madison
Flanagan, Alice K. *Dolley Payne Todd Madison.* New York: Children's Press, 1997.

Molly Pitcher
Bertanzetti, Eileen Dunn. *Molly Pitcher: Heroine.* Philadelphia: Chelsea House Publishers, 2002.

Paul Revere
Sullivan, George. *Paul Revere.* New York: Scholastic Reference, 2000.

George Washington
Marrin, Albert. *George Washington and the Founding of a Nation.* New York: Dutton Children's Books, 2001.

Zachary Taylor
Kent, Zachary. *Zachary Taylor: Twelfth President of the United States.* Chicago: Children's Press, 1998.

VIDEOS

Benjamin Franklin. PBS, 2002. (DVD)
Founding Brothers. A&E Home Video, 2002. (DVD)
Founding Fathers. The History Channel/A&E Television Networks, 2000. (Videocassette)
Liberty—The American Revolution. PBS, 2004. (DVD)
Rebels and Redcoats—How Britain Lost America. PBS, 2004. (DVD)

WEB SITES

John Adams
http://www.whitehouse.gov/history/presidents/ja2.html
A biography of John Adams; Web site is maintained by the White House
http://ap.grolier.com/article?assetid=0002340-0&templatename=/article/article.html
Encyclopedia entry

John Quincy Adams
http://www.whitehouse.gov/history/presidents/ja6.html
Biography of John Quincy Adams; Web site is maintained by the White House
http://ap.grolier.com/article?assetid=0002360-0&templatename=/article/article.html
Encyclopedia entry

Samuel Adams
http://www.whitehouse.gov/kids/dreamteam/samueladams.html
A biography of Samuel Adams with study questions

African American Patriots

http://www.crispusattucks.org/crispus_attucks.html
   A biography of Crispus Attucks
http://www.infoplease.com/ipa/A0886828.html
   A biography of James Armistead Lafayette
http://www.rootsweb.com/~nwa/mammy.html
   A story of Mammy Kate and Stephen Heard

Ethan Allen and the Green Mountain Boys

http://www.americanrevwar.homestead.com/files/ALLEN.HTM
   A biography of Ethan Allen
http://www.bartleby.com/65/al/Allen-Et.html
   Encyclopedia entry

The Constitution of the United States of America

http://www.constitutionfacts.com/cbody2.shtml
   Facts about the Constitution
http://www.common-place.org/vol-02/no-04/tales
   Information about opening the vault in which the Constitution was sealed

Margaret Cochran Corbin

http://www.distinguishedwomen.com/biographies/corbin.html
   A biography of Margaret Corbin
http://www.muzzleblasts.com/vol3no4/articles/mbo34-3.html
   A biography of Margaret Corbin and information on the Petticoat Patriots

George Rogers Clark

http://www.historycarper.com/kids/htfah/grclark.htm
   A biography of George Rogers Clark

Culper Ring

http://www.odci.gov/cia/publications/warindep/pers.shtml
   Information from the Central Intelligence Agency about spies during the Revolutionary War

Lydia Darragh and the Daughters of Liberty

http://www.ushistory.org/march/bio/lydia.htm
   A biography of Lydia Darragh

The Declaration of Independence

http://www.loc.gov/exhibits/declara/declara1.html
   A Web site for the Library of Congress; information about drafting the Declaration, the library's exhibit about the declaration, and a chronology of events surrounding the signing of the Declaration of Independence
http://www.ushistory.org/declaration
   A Web site with the text of the declaration, information about the signers of the declaration, and Thomas Jefferson's own account about writing the declaration

Drummers and Fifers

http://www.revwar75.com/library/rees/musician1.htm
   Information on drums, fifes, and music in the Continental army
http://bands.army.mil/history/firstarmyregulation.asp
   Information on army bands and Baron Friedrich von Steuben

Benjamin Edes

http://www.famousamericans.net/benjaminedes
   A biography of Benjamin Edes

Benjamin Franklin

http://www.english.udel.edu/lemay/franklin
   A biography of Benjamin Franklin
http://www.incwell.com/Biographies/Franklin.html
   A biography of Benjamin Franklin with links to his autobiography

Bernardo de Gálvez

http://www.lasculturas.com/aa/bio/bioBernardoGalvez.php
   A biography of Bernardo de Gálvez
http://www.tsha.utexas.edu/handbook/online/articles/view/GG/fga10.html
   A biography of Bernardo de Gálvez; Web site is maintained by the University of Texas

Deborah Samson Gannett

http://www.canton.org/samson
   A biography of Deborah Samson Gannett
http://www.geocities.com/Heartland/Plains/1789/samson.html
   A biography of Deborah Samson Gannett

Emily Geiger

http://sciway3.net/clark/revolutionarywar/geiger13.html
   The legend of Emily Geiger
http://sciway3.net/clark/revolutionarywar/geiger21.html
   Story of the relics of Emily Geiger

George Gibson

http://www.qmfound.com/COL_George_Gibson.html
   A biography of Colonel George Gibson
http://www.qmfound.com
   Web site for the Army Quartermaster Foundation, with stories of quartermaster history
   and traditions, and biographies of famous quartermasters

Mary Katherine Goddard

http://www.mdarchives.state.md.us/msa/educ/exhibits/womenshall/html/goddard.html
   A Web site for Maryland Women's Hall of Fame
http://www.onlinewbc.gov/whm_mkgmg.html
   A Web site maintained by the Small Business Administration about women in business

Nathanael Greene

http://www.ushistory.org/valleyforge/served/greene.html
    A biography of Nathanael Greene
http://www.qmfound.com/greene.htm
    A biography of Nathanael Greene; Web site is maintained by the Quartermaster Foundation

Nathan Hale

http://www.ctssar.org/patriots/nathan_hale.htm
    A biography of Nathan Hale; Web site is maintained by The Connecticut Society of the Sons of the American Revolution
http://www.newsday.com/community/guide/lihistory/ny-history-hs413a,0, 6240190.story
    A biography of Nathan Hale; Web site about Long Island and its history

Alexander Hamilton

http://www.jmu.edu/madison/center/main_pages/madison_archives/era/parties/power/hamilton.htm
    A biography of Alexander Hamilton
http://www.isidore-of-seville.com/hamilton
    A Web site devoted to Alexander Hamilton containing links to biographies, Hamilton's writings, and books about Hamilton

John Hancock

http://www.ushistory.org/declaration/signers/hancock.htm
    A biography of John Hancock
http://www.rebelswithavision.com/JohnHancock.org
    A biography of John Hancock

Mary Hays McCauley

http://sill-www.army.mil/pao/pamolly.htm
    The story of Molly Pitcher
http://search.eb.com/women/articles/Pitcher_Molly.html
    A biography of Molly Pitcher

Patrick Henry

http://www.history.org/Almanack/people/bios/biohen.cfm
    A biography of Patrick Henry
http://www.ushistory.org/declaration/related/henry.htm
    A biography of Patrick Henry with links to other resources
http://theamericanrevolution.org/ipeople/phenry.asp
    A biography of Patrick Henry with recommended readings

Sam Houston

http://www.tsha.utexas.edu/handbook/online/articles/view/HH/fho73.html
    A biography of Sam Houston
http://www.shsu.edu/~smm_www/History/index.html
    A time line for the life of Sam Houston

Andrew Jackson

http://www.americanpresident.org/history/andrewjackson/
   A biography of Andrew Jackson
http://www.whitehouse.gov/history/presidents/aj7.html
   A biography of Andrew Jackson; Web site is maintained by the White House

John Jay

http://usgovinfo.about.com/library/weekly/aa081400a.htm
   A history of the U.S. Supreme Court
http://www.ushistory.org/declaration/related/jay.htm
   A biography of John Jay

Thomas Jefferson

http://www.whitehouse.gov/history/presidents/tj3.html
   A biography of Thomas Jefferson; Web site is maintained by the White House
http://ap.grolier.com/article?assetid=0152900-0&templatename=/article/article.html
   Encyclopedia entry

Jewish Patriots

http://www.jewishworldreview.com/jewish/salvador.asp
   A biography of Francis Salvador
http://www.borisamericanjews.org
   A Web site about an exhibit on American Jewish history, including patriots in the Revolutionary War

John Paul Jones

http://www.seacoastnh.com/Maritime_History/John_Paul_Jones/John_Paul_Jones/
   Web site dedicated to John Paul Jones containing several articles about different times in Jones's life
http://www.chinfo.navy.mil/navpalib/traditions/html/jpjones.html
   A story of John Paul Jones's naval battles; Web site is maintained by the U.S. Navy

Jack Jouett

http://www.louisacounty.com/jouett.htm
   A biography of Jack Jouett
http://www.americanrevolution.org/jouett.html
   A biography of Jack Jouett and the story of the "other ride"

Henry Knox

http://www.generalknoxmuseum.org/knoxbio.html
   A biography of Henry Knox; Web site is maintained by the General Knox Museum
http://www.ushistory.org/valleyforge/served/knox.html
   A biography of Henry Knox

Tadeusz Kosciuszko

http://www.lituanus.org/1986/86_1_03.htm
    A biography of Tadeusz Kosciuszko

The Marquis de Lafayette

http://www.ushistory.org/valleyforge/served/lafayette.html
    A biography of the Marquis de Lafayette
http://www.flssar.org/lafayett.html
    A biography of the Marquis de Lafayette

Richard Henry Lee

http://www.colonialhall.com/leerh/leerh.php
    A biography of Richard Henry Lee
http://www.stratfordhall.org/richardh.html
    A biography of the Lees of Virginia

Liberty Bell

http://www.ushistory.org/libertybell
    A history of the Liberty Bell
http://www.nps.gov/inde/liberty-bell.html
    Information about the Liberty Bell

Sybil Ludington

http://www.catskill.net/purple/sybil.htm
    A biography of Sybil Ludington
http://www.mahopaclibrary.org/localhistory/sybil_ludington.htm
    Excerpts from *Sybil Ludington: Heroine of the Revolutionary War, Alive and Well at 220 Years Old* by V.T. Dacquino; Web site is maintained by the Mahopac Library

Dolley Madison

http://www.madisonbrigade.com/library_jm_d_madison.htm
    A biography of Dolley Madison
http://www.lkwdpl.org/wihohio/madi-dol.htm
    A biography of Dolley Madison

James Madison

http://www.madisonbrigade.com/library_jm.htm#BIOGRAPHY
    A biography of James Madison
http://ap.grolier.com/article?assetid=0181210-0&templatename=article/article.html
    Encyclopedia entry

Francis Marion

http://encarta.msn.com/encyclopedia_761558037/Marion_Francis.html
    Encyclopedia entry

George Mason

http://odur.let.rug.nl/~usa/B/gmason/gmasxx.htm
A biography of George Mason

http://www.gunstonhall.org/revolution
A biography of George Mason

James Monroe

http://ap.grolier.com/article?assetid=0197240-0&templatename=/article/article.html
Encyclopedia entry

http://www.whitehouse.gov/history/presidents/jm5.html
A biography of James Monroe; Web site is maintained by the White House

Robert Morris

http://www.robert-morris.com
Web site about Robert Morris

http://www.libertystory.net/LSACTIONROBERTMORRIS.htm
A biography of Robert Morris

Oneida Indians

http://ca.essortment.com/oneidairoquois_rjay.htm
A history of the Oneida Indians and their role in the Battle of Oriskany

http://www.oneida-nation.net/oskan2.html
A biography of Chief Oskanondonha, one of the Oneida heroes

James Otis

http://www.barnstablepatriot.com/sscape/jotis.html
A biography of James Otis

http://encarta.msn.com/encyclopedia_761574427/Otis_James.html
Encyclopedia entry

Thomas Paine

http://odur.let.rug.nl/~usa/B/tpaine/paine.htm
A biography of Thomas Paine

Publius

http://www.constitution.org/fed/federa00.htm
A brief introduction to THE FEDERALIST PAPERS, with text from each essay

Casimir Pulaski

http://www.newadvent.org/cathen/12561a.htm
Encyclopedia entry

http://www.newbedford.k12.ma.us/elementary/casimir.htm
A biography of Casimir Pulaski

The Purple Heart

http://www.purpleheart.org/history.htm
The history of the Purple Heart

http://www.purpleheart.org/Awd_of_PH.htm
An explanation of how a member of the armed services is awarded a Purple Heart

Paul Revere
http://www.ctssar.org/patriots/paul_revere.htm
A biography of Paul Revere; Web site is maintained by the Connecticut Society of the Sons of the American Revolution
http://www.americanrevolution.org/revere.html
Paul Revere's own account of his ride

Caesar Rodney
http://www.state.de.us/facts/history/rodnbio.htm
Web site about Delaware and its heroes
http://www.ushistory.org/declaration/signers/rodney.htm
A biography of Caesar Rodney

Betsy Ross
http://www.usflag.org/about.betsy.ross.html
A story about the legend of Betsy Ross
http://www.ushistory.org/betsy/flaglife.html
A biography of Betsy Ross

Benjamin Rush
http://chronicles.dickinson.edu/encyclo/r/ed_rushB.html
A biography of Benjamin Rush
http://server1.fandm.edu/departments/benrush/ben.html
A Web site maintained by the Benjamin Rush Society at Franklin and Marshall University

Sequoyah
http://ngeorgia.com/people/sequoyah.html
A biography of Sequoyah
http://www.sequoyahmuseum.org/
A biography of Sequoyah

Roger Sherman
http://www.ctssar.org
Web site for the Connecticut Society of the Sons of the American Revolution; gives information on Connecticut patriots and a month-by-month history of the American Revolution
http://www.colonialhall.com/sherman/sherman.php
Web site for Colonial Hall; contains biographies of all signers of the Declaration of Independence

Baron Friedrich von Steuben
http://www.ushistory.org/valleyforge/served/steuben.html
A biography of Baron Friedrich von Steuben

"The Star-Spangled Banner"

http://www.softdata.co.uk/gloucester/smith.htm
A biography of John Stafford Smith
http://www.law.ou.edu/hist/ssb.html
All four verses of the "The Star-Spangled Banner"

Zachary Taylor

http://ap.grolier.com/article?assetid=0285260-0&templatename=/article/article.html
Encyclopedia entry
http://www.whitehouse.gov/history/presidents/zt12.html
A biography of President Zachary Taylor; Web site is maintained by the White House

Dr. James Thacher

http://footguards.tripod.com/08HISTORY/08_thacher.htm
A profile of Dr. Thacher and excerpts from his journals

Charles Thomson

http://greatseal.com/committees/finaldesign/
The story of Charles Thomson and the Great Seal of the United States

John Trumbull

http://www.nga.gov/cgi-bin/pbio?30800
A biography of John Trumbull
http://earlyamerica.com/review/summer/trumbull.html
A story about John Trumbull, the artist of the Revolution

Mercy Otis Warren

http://www.masshist.org/bh/mercybio.html
A biography of Mercy Otis Warren; Web site is maintained by the Massachusetts Historical Society

George Washington

http://www.whitehouse.gov/history/presidents/gw1.html
A biography of George Washington; Web site is maintained by the White House
http://ap.grolier.com/article?assetid=0307840-0&templatename=/article/article.html
Encyclopedia entry

Anthony Wayne

http://virtualology.com/anthonywayne.org
A biography of Anthony Wayne
http://www.bbc.co.uk/dna/h2g2/A219791
A story about Anthony Wayne's ghost

INDEX

Numbers in *italics* represent illustrations.

PHOTO CREDITS

Photographs © 2005: Alan McGowen: 194, 230; American Jewish Historical Society, Newton Centre, Massachusetts and New York, New York: 218, 219; American Philosophical Society Library, Philadelphia: cover bottom left, 11; Architect of the Capitol, Washington, DC: 170; Art Resource, NY: back cover bottom left, 75 (James Barton Longacre/National Portrait Gallery, Smithsonian Institution, Washington, DC, USA), 226 (Frank Blackwell Mayer/Smithsonian American Art Museum, Washington, DC, USA), 16, 182 (National Portrait Gallery, Smithsonian Institution, Washington, DC, USA), cover top right, 57 (Gilbert Stuart/Private Collection); Bridgeman Art Library International Ltd., London/New York: 173 (Asher Brown Durand/ Private Collection/The Stapleton Collection), back cover bottom right, back cover center right, 99, 168 (New-York Historical Society, New York, USA), 175 (John Trumbull/Museum of Fine Arts, Boston, Massachusetts, USA/Gift of Howland S. Warren); Corbis Images: 250 (Nathan Benn), cover bottom right, 1, 24, 39, 41, 83, 87, 116, 126, 142, 150, 157, 178, 246 (Bettmann), 120 (A. Girard), 134 (Bob Krist), 81 (Royalty-Free), 235, 257 (Joseph Sohm/Visions of America), 198 (The Corcoran Gallery of Art); Courtesy of the Danbury Museum and Historical Society: 190; Getty Images/Hulton Archive: cover bottom center, 211 (Archive Photos), cover top left, 34 (Kean Collection), 28, 95 (MPI), 108 (Stock Montage), 49, 53, 243; Jack Jouett House: 154; Library of Congress: 253 (Matthew Brady), 31, 159, 202; Maryland State Archives: 91; Museum of Fine Arts, Boston: 20 (Deposited by the City of Boston, Samuel Adams, about 1722, by John Singleton Copley, American, 1738–1815, 30.76c), back cover top right, 70 (Gift of Joseph W. Revere, William B. Revere, and Edward H.R. Revere, 30.781); North Wind Picture Archives: back cover top left, 22, 37, 43, 45, 62, 73, 79, 104, 130, 164, 186, 215, 240; Photo Researchers, NY/Tom McHugh/National Portrait Gallery, Wash., DC: 66; Pilgrim Hall Museum, Plymouth, MA: 160; Sam Houston Memorial Museum, Huntsville, TX: 265; Stock Montage, Inc.: back cover left center, cover top center, 112, 123, 146, 207, 262; Superstock, Inc.: 13 (John Ward Dunsmore), 132 (Metropolitan Museum of Art, New York City); The Image Works/color by Laura Wiley: 89; U.S. Army Quartermaster Museum: 222; U.S. Army Women's Museum, Fort Lee, VA/Jerry Burgess: 138.

Copyright extends to corresponding image on Contents page.

ABOUT THE AUTHOR

Nancy Robinson Masters is the author of sixteen books, including *The Airplane*, a title in the Inventions That Shaped the World series published by Franklin Watts. She is also the author of *Georgia* and *Kansas* in America, the Beautiful, second series.

Nancy's passion for instilling patriotism in young readers has been recognized by the U.S. Air Force, which twice honored her with the Distinguished Citizen of the Year award for her efforts.

In addition to writing books, Nancy is a pilot, and a full-time freelance journalist whose articles, essays, stories, and poems appear in a variety of publications. She is a frequent speaker at schools, civic groups, and professional organizations, promoting the power of reading and writing in a free society. Her travels as a journalist have taken her around the world, including Antarctica as a guest of the National Science Foundation.

Nancy's writing room is in the home she and her husband, veteran aviator Bill Masters, share with their three cats and four dogs in the Elmdale community near Abilene, Texas.